VALUES, ETHICS & FAILURE
IN THE DIGITAL AGE

Howard A. Tullman

Values, Ethics & Failure in the Digital Age
Copyright © 2017 by Howard A. Tullman. All rights reserved.

No part of this publication may be reproduced, stored in a retrieval system or transmitted in any way by any means, electronic, mechanical, photocopy, recording or otherwise without the prior permission of the author except as provided by USA copyright law.

Published in the United States of America
For bulk orders, please contact info@blogintobook.com

Cover design portrait courtesy of Matthew Cherry
Perspiration Principles logo designed by James "Red" Schmitt
Special Thanks to Lakshmi Shenoy, Colleen Maxwell and Claudia Saric

To purchase all volumes of The Perspiration Principles, please visit:
BlogIntoBook.com/tullman/
ISBN: 9781619849716

DEDICATION

Sitting down every week to write something that will be meaningful and ideally of lasting value to others is a lot like setting out to start a new business. Sometimes there's a germ of an idea; sometimes it's an emotional reaction or other driver; or perhaps it's just a problem or situation that needs to be addressed. And occasionally you simply want to see things change and no one else is stepping up to the plate to make that happen.

You can't know how hard, long or costly (in many ways) the journey will be and there are no guarantees that anything good will ever come of your efforts, but you know for certain that nothing will ever happen if you don't get the process started and try. It's a lonely path and every bit of encouragement, assistance and support that you find along the way makes the job a little easier and slightly more likely to succeed.

I hope that these books will be my modest contribution to your success and to the well-worn and tattered bag of hopes and dreams which we call entrepreneurship.

CONTENTS

Part I – Values And Ethics

Back To Basics – Startup 101 9
Situational Ethics Suck... 13
Tricked Traffic Isn't Worth The Trouble.. 17
There's No Excuse For Being A Tech Jerk 21
Keep Raising The Bar 25
You Can't Add Value If You Don't Have Values.................................... 29
Sometimes Enough Is Enough 35
It Helps To Know Where You're Headed 39
How To Talk Yourself Out Of A Job 45
Why Rabbits Don't Run Big Businesses 51
Networking Tips From The Top 55
Snapchat – Saying It Doesn't Make It So 59
Do My Steps Count If My Fitbit Isn't Counting Them? 63
Be The One They Can Count On 67
A/B Testing Is So Yesterday – And So's Your Mba............................... 73
Fence It And Forget It... 79
It's Really Hard To Hide In Plain Sight 85
Ignorance Masquerading As Opinion... 89
You Don't Know Shinola 93
Are Entrepreneurs Born Or Built Or Both? 97
What Our Kids Should Learn In School 101
Silicon Wadi Documentary 107
If You Can Do It, It Ain't Braggin'... 111
Why Entrepreneurs Are Really Terrible At Saying Thank You 115
Startup Lessons From Super Bowl 50... 119

Part II – Failure

What Nobody Tells You About Failure 125
Failure Happens. Four Rules For Doing It Well 133
Forget About Failing Fast. If You Must, Fail Forward Instead 137
Make Cheap Mistakes 141
Don't Waste Your Time Chasing Perfect 147
It's Not About Failing, It's About Scaling 153
Two Words Every Innovator Should Know 157
Take A Hard Look At Why Your Stuff Isn't Selling 163
Brene Brown At 1871 For A Fireside Chat 169
First Things First – Family And Friends 175
Even Superman Gets Sad Sometimes 179
Seven Scars Make An Entrepreneur 183
About The Author 191

PART I

Values and Ethics

BACK TO BASICS - STARTUP 101

I spoke recently on business basics at the Chicago Startup Summit which was put together by the terrific teams at Virgin Unite and RM72 as an educational and networking experience for entrepreneurs (and wannabes as well) with a particular focus on socially-conscious businesses. The day-long event was held at Chicago's new Virgin Hotel which is especially near and dear to my heart because: (a) it's pretty much a startup itself - being that it is the first Virgin Hotel in the world with 20 more to come and (b) the core team which put the new property together did their initial ideation and development as active members and residents of 1871.

When I ordinarily talk about The Perspiration Principles, I try to focus on what I regard as the 5 main requirements for success in business and, of course, in life as well: passion, preparation, perspiration, perseverance and principles (or values). The sessions at the Summit were an opportunity to broaden the conversation and add three more P's to the pot: a focus also on people, purpose and planet.

The central idea was how we can change businesses for good either by creating businesses that specifically focus on doing good or helping existing businesses think about (and actually implement) cost-effective and innovative ways that they can do their business in a better fashion which takes into account broader concerns and the idea of a double bottom line.

The diverse group of speakers and presenters I joined spanned the entire social spectrum so much so that I felt from time to time that - while I was talking about bedrock basics - super-smart people like Mats Lederhausen were talking about concepts and ideas that sounded a lot more like rocket science. But based on the reactions and comments of the crowd, everybody found something to help them make sense of this crazy and exciting new world of constant change and disruptive innovation.

In any event, I was grateful for the opportunity to review with the group some of the basic ideas and strategies that have been the foundation for almost half a century now of my practice and of The Perspiration Principles as well. While some of the ideas have been expanded and adapted, it is amazing how little the fundamental premises have varied. Many of them are self-explanatory and where they aren't I've just added a short summary.

Here are the Top 10 from my ever-growing list:

1. You Get What You Work for, Not What You Wish For

Hard work always wins. In the real world, effort trumps talent. Hope is not a strategy. We may not outsmart them all, but we'll certainly outwork them.

2. Keep Raising the Bar

Constant iteration is the key. You get better by getting better. Successive approximation beats postponed perfection. There's no finish line – ever.

3. Shoot for the Stars

Always ask for the best seat in the house. You miss 100% of the shots you don't take. If you don't ask, the answer's always "no".

4. Don't Sell Yourself Short

Feasibility will compromise you soon enough. Don't allow yourself to be defined by the limitations of other people. Fueling your fears is a waste of imagination.

5. Keep Moving Forward

Excellence is always anchored in perseverance. It's only a "No" for now. Over every hill is another hill. The only easy day was yesterday.

6. Start Now with What You Have

Waiting doesn't necessarily get you to a better answer. The time will never be "just right". Elaboration in planning is a form of pollution. A good plan executed today beats a perfect plan next week. It's easier to ask for forgiveness than permission. Only the winners decide what were the war crimes.

7. Nobody Said Life Was Fair

In the world of startups, there aren't rewards or punishments, there are only consequences. Some win, some lose, but those who don't constantly change, die for sure. There's no such thing as a good excuse. Make smart mistakes and don't repeat them.

8. Never Play the Blame Game

People who blame their circumstances for their situation will never change things for the better. The ones who succeed look for the conditions they need to succeed and – if they can't find them – they make them.

When you continually blame others, you give up your power to make things better.

9. Sometimes the Baby is Just Ugly

Time is the scarcest resource. Opportunity costs are everything. If you're digging yourself into a hole, the first order of business is to stop digging. Don't be reluctant to change your mind. Don't try to do things cheaply that you shouldn't be doing at all. Stubborn on vision; flexible on details.

10. Make Something that Makes a Difference

Focus on making a difference and making a life rather than just trying to make a living.

SITUATIONAL ETHICS SUCK

I'm afraid that we're developing another generation gap and this one isn't merely cosmetic (can't stand those tattoos!) or aurally aesthetic (can't stand that music!) or even extreme economic (why "own" anything). It's far more important than any of these fairly superficial differences and preferences – albeit I recognize that they are crushingly important to the hosts of *TMZ* and *Access Hollywood*.

And it's far more pressing and critical than the angst and quasi-parental concerns these weird choices engender in us grown-ups. I can deal with all the questionable choices that many young people are making today because I'm relatively sure that we all made similar (or much worse, but probably less long-lasting) choices in our youth and yet, amazingly enough, we're still here, standing tall, and giving them advice and the "benefit" of our wisdom – such as it is.

But I'm not talking about something that's a preference or an option that we can take or leave – I'm talking about a problem that threatens to undermine something so fundamental and basic to the conduct of business (and especially to early-stage angel investing) that almost everyone (other than those in the film or music business) has always taken it for gospel and for granted. They say every day in the film business, "I'll love you 'til I don't" so get used to it. But that kind of fleeting attachment or commitment and the complete absence of sincerity that's "just business" in those worlds isn't the way we hope and expect that the rest of the sane (and square) business world conducts itself.

That's why I'm getting increasingly concerned about this very basic idea. I recently heard Alan Matthew (a long-time successful options and commodities trader) express it forcefully in about 15 different ways throughout a recent talk he gave to several hundred entrepreneurs at 1871. He said that, in every deal he does, and in every transaction: "My word is my bond." And it's just that simple – especially in the trading pits in Chicago – where the entire ecosystem depends on trust and the ability for everyone to rely on the commitments and honesty of the other players. But the problem is that - even as essential a part as this attitude is to how we do business in Chicago - I don't think we're doing a good job of communicating this very critical concept to today's young entrepreneurs. Too many of them live in a different conceptual world – one driven by situational ethics. And it sucks.

Telling people half the story or what they want to hear instead of what they need to hear isn't a funding solution – it's an invitation to a later slaughter. And it's usually the entrepreneur and the management team who will ultimately get killed. So it makes sense to share ALL of the news all the time – if for no other reason than to just save yourself all the grief coming down the line. The truth never hurts unless it ought to and sometimes it's a powerful wake-up call for all concerned. There's never a really good or special time to decide to tell the truth – the time is all the time.

But, if you haven't been there (to make the right choice regardless of how hard or discouraging it may be or how it may impact your financing or prospects) and there's no one more experienced around to guide you because you're running full-speed ahead and you're also making it up as you go, it's far too easy to take a quick slide down that slippery ethical slope. And once you lose someone's confidence, once they come to believe that you don't share and abide by their fundamental values, you will never get their trust and support entirely back.

And, honestly, because a whole generation of kids have been told (at least since second grade) that they're amazing, exceptional and completely unique, it's just a short step for them to conclude that the ordinary rules don't apply to them and that morals are just for little people and that they're way above that somewhat mundane conformity and far too smart for it as well. An old friend of mine used to say – by way of excusing virtually anything disgusting that he managed to do - that exceptional people deserve special concessions. I'm afraid his disease may be spreading.

As I often <u>kiddingly</u> say when I'm talking about building your company's culture and instilling critical values in your people and your business processes: "These are my principles. If you don't like them, I have others." But that's always intended as a joke because – in the real world – we don't get to pick and choose when to honor our promises and commitments. We say what we'll do and then we do what we said we'd do. It couldn't be more straightforward – you don't get to be truthful some of the time or some time later or when it's a better or more convenient time. The truth doesn't vary based on circumstances.

And frankly, I'm not even sure that, in some cases, this is purely an issue of intentional dishonesty or immorality. I think it's just as much a lack of experience and education combined with way too much enthusiasm. Entrepreneurs can talk themselves into anything (I call this the "that hooker really liked me" condition) and, once they do, they want to sell it to the world. But whenever you find that you're having to shade the truth or forget some ugly facts in order to convince yourself or talk your team or some investor into something that you're not even sure you yourself buy off on, you're probably not doing yourself or anyone else a favor. It's almost inevitably a bad deal which you should back away from as quickly as possible.

And, while it's great to be highly motivated, it's not even a little cool if no one trusts your motives. It takes a time and hard work to build any kind of relationship, but just an instant and a suspicion (a long way from proof) to destroy it. And I know just how hard it is to say things that no one wants to hear, but that's part of the leader's job – it's not delegable and it's not optional.

It takes a great deal of experience and a whole bunch of broken dreams and busted relationships to appreciate that to be trusted is a much greater compliment than to be loved. Entrepreneurs – without a doubt – need and want (first and foremost) to be loved. It's part of the sickness which drives us. But, at the end of the day, trust is the only thing that you can really take to the bank.

TRICKED TRAFFIC ISN'T WORTH THE TROUBLE

An age-old question. If a tree falls in the forest, but there's no one there to hear it, does it make a sound? Who knows and who really cares? The better and more pressing question these days is: if the primary drivers for traffic to a website that you're paying money to advertise on are hacks, tricks and clever pet pix; what are the visitors who do show up (even assuming they are people and not tracking robots) really worth to you or anybody else?

I'd argue that they're not worth your time and certainly not worth any money you're paying for the very modest privilege of "entertaining" (in the loosest sense of the word) a bunch of morons with nothing better to do than to waste their time randomly clicking on just about anything. Instead of attracting people who might actually be interested in your products or services and also highly influential, you can end up spending money to attract mobs of easily-influenced people instead who probably couldn't explain how they go to the website if they were asked.

One of the things I always told restaurant owners about *Groupon* daily deals was that they were designed to attract "cheapies" to restaurants that were only looking for one-time deals instead of "foodies" who could become regular patrons and the true lifeblood of the business. And since I'm from Chicago and everyone's picking on *Groupon* these days, let me just say that we use it and that it makes sense for a lot of different kinds of businesses and situations IF you keep in mind 4 basic rules about when to do a daily-deals kind of deal:

1. The deal needs to drive new users and incremental revenue – not replace or cannibalize existing full margin revenues;

2. Your business can't be subject to capacity or size constraints which might result in the incremental traffic precluding access by and for existing customers and users;

3. The deal can't require you to spend or invest a great deal of upfront money with essentially sunk costs if the deal doesn't go; and

4. You can't put yourself in a position where taking on and delivering the deal gives you cash flow or other float problems.

But *Groupon* deals aside, there are still way too many companies "buying" into tonnage and volume (quantity rather than quality) and measuring their results by the wrong competitive metrics like "likes" and followers. As a result, the market continues to encourage young entrepreneurs to create (or basically make up) businesses which are all about buzz and bullshit rather than trying to build sustainable businesses which deliver real services and demonstrable results to clients and which have concrete economic rewards for those companies rather than cosmetic and superficial results that do nothing for any business's bottom line.

I keep seeing and hearing pitches and presentations predicated on prevarications, phony postings, and a pile of pictures that may be inexplicably popular, but have nothing really to do with anything and clearly nothing whatsoever to do with your products, services or business. As an example, I just sat through a highly-energized, but essentially empty, "presentation" about content and engagement which sadly, instead of being about ideas and approaches of substance, was all about scams and slick, but sleazy ploys to trick people into being traffic to sites for no good reason. A load of tactics and no real strategy or smarts. Or maybe they were really being just a little <u>too</u> smart for their own ultimate good. Because even if you're the biggest and fastest rat in the race, when the dust settles, you're still pretty much a rat.

THERE'S NO EXCUSE FOR BEING A TECH JERK

The need to scale a business quickly doesn't give you leeway to abuse people or act any way other than appropriately. That's why it's important to establish the right values on Day One.

These aren't the best of times for the tech industry. Every day another jerk emerges as the latest poster boy of ego and entitlement, someone who can't figure out how to keep his hands to himself and/or his ugly mouth shut. And the many feeble attempts and faux justifications made in the name of speed and scale doesn't really advance the discussion or explain the situation, either.

It's as if we're saying that, because we're in such a hurry to be huge, we don't have the time to be decent human beings. Come on, there have to be some basic behavioral ground rules and a little more substance to the culture of the tech and entrepreneurial community than the celebration of cash, cars, and creepy, chauvinistic CEOs chugging Cristal. I get that money doesn't care whose pockets it ends up in, but morals and menschkeit actually do matter.

And I also realize that, apart from the obvious and easy cases of gross and overt behavior, it's not quite as simple as you might think to create some guidelines and guard rails for these situations. One issue is that many of these businesses are being built and run by beginners. As often as not, they're no more advanced and informed in terms of their people strengths and skills than they are in any of the other areas of operating and growing a business. You can tell people things over and over again until you run out of breath, but ultimately you can't understand for them. If they don't get it and take these ideas to heart, the job just doesn't get done.

It gets even more complicated when you try to put a stake in the ground and commit your team to certain important ideas and values. Because in the real world, even the most sacrosanct values are somewhat mutable. And in the context of an immature business, some of them actually do have to change-- at least from a priority perspective-- as time passes and the organization grows and hopefully matures. There are concerns and necessities that drive the operations of a startup (like making payroll and keeping the doors open) that aren't the same as those which a larger and more established company can "afford." Survival in the short run sometimes trumps the desire and ability to secure other social goals. Even if your heart is 100% in the right place, it's hard when you're in a hurry to serve too many different masters or to try to be all things to everyone.

Democracy in decision making is a good, simple example. It's absolutely clear that whatever the "deal" was when the startup got started about everyone being consulted and having a vote on every important decision, it doesn't usually last beyond the first fundraising. There's just not enough room at the table for everyone to have a seat. And, more importantly, too many things become time-sensitive to let you take the time to take everyone's temperature on every question. There are solid business reasons, as the size and complexity of your business increases, to avoid inviting everyone to every party.

But none of these legitimate considerations excuse the plain old boorish behaviors or worse that we're reading about today. No entrepreneur can afford to create a company culture that isn't based on certain fundamental beliefs established right at the start of the enterprise. It's a lot easier from Day One to live up to 100% of your values than 99% because there's no end to that slippery slope once you begin to move in that direction. And you never know how deep your commitment really is until those values are stress tested. Talk is cheap.

If you build a business based exclusively on speed and shortcuts-- even if you claim to be acting in the best interests of your customers-- you'll eventually end up with a second-rate solution. If your best idea is always to blame the customer and never take responsibility for the cause and the remedy, your products and services will surely and shortly suck. Worst of all, if you encourage your people to embellish the truth or flat out lie to your customers, they'll eventually lie to you, too. Fish and businesses rot from the head down. There's a right way-;not necessarily an easy way-;to do these things, but it starts at the top of the organization.

And when you do get it right and your culture is clicking on all cylinders, it's a beautiful thing. That's why it's especially encouraging for me to occasionally stumble upon a story worth sharing that suggests there are still people in our business who actually give a damn about the things that really matter.

This is one such tale. We were in a board meeting for one of our EdTech companies and talking about the usual KPIs and basic business stuff and about how various aspects of the company's product development and enhancement efforts were progressing-- especially how quickly we were moving to bring some of these new and critical features to market. Remember that July's an especially tough and stressful time in the EdTech world because the start of the new school year is just around the corner and, if you're not there when the doors open, you're nowhere.

You spend a lot of time in these meetings dealing with the "nice to have" versus the "need to have" issues. There's often a lot of jargon and abbreviations in these "technical" conversations. It appeared to me that one major set of fixes and updates (which had been a gating factor for a lot of the work to follow, and consumed a lot of time and resources) was nearly complete. That would allow the developers to move on to the next changes, which were clearly revenue and student acquisition drivers.

And here's where the conversation got really interesting. The just-finished changes weren't gonna add students any time soon. They weren't going to drive new monthly or quarterly revenues. They weren't even being requested or required by current customers, who were basically happy with the status quo. Under the best of scenarios, the changes addressed to the needs of only a tiny portion of the potential user population.

This didn't feel like either "need" or "nice" to have-- it felt like the last place the team should be spending scarce resources or critical time. In fact, it turns out that there's another category in the consideration set for companies that care about what they're doing and why. It's called "right to have". What were the changes all about? They all related to upgrades in ADA-compliant accessibility. Keyboard capabilities, screen readers, and captioning - all necessary to make the company's products available and workable for everyone. Changes that were anticipatory and miles and miles ahead of the market, most of the competition, and even their own users. And, make no mistake, this was heavy lifting and a lot of thankless hard work.

Bottom line: Not necessarily the place that the numbers or non-stop notoriety would ever take you, but the right thing to do if you're trying to make an important difference in people's lives.

KEEP RAISING THE BAR

The hyper-competitive world we now live in is full of fast followers. In our constantly-connected world of instantaneous information, every new business immediately spawns copy-cats, riffers, and discounters as well as cheap knock-offs and old-line traditional players trying to use their brands and their bigness to barge right into these new markets. Most of the low-end guys quickly learn to their dismay that no one wins the race to the bottom and that, in today's economy, even "free" isn't cheap enough in most cases because smart shoppers are increasingly jealous and careful with their time and their resources. Today's consumer rallying cry could well be "give me something of real value or give me a break and get out of my face".

Because the barriers to entry keep shrinking, it's just as easy for the next 5 guys to start a business like yours as it was for you. In fact, in many cases, when you invent and establish a new product, service, sector or approach, you actually make it easier for the guys running right behind you to succeed.

First of all, they ride on your coattails, your PR and your advertising in every possible way to explain their business. They're not pioneers breaking new ground; they're not inventing anything; they've just learned to say "we're just like X but cheaper or faster or closer", etc. Saying "we're just like Groupon but better" saves a shitload of time, money and marketing.

Second, they lean on your progress and success to establish their own credibility and to show their customers that the thing works and works well.

And third, they go to school on your errors and missteps so they save time and money by avoiding first-timer mistakes and by entering the product development and delivery cycle at a much more advanced and higher (as well as more stable) level than you did. The questions are so much easier when someone else has already worked out the right answers for you.

The fact is that while the barriers to real success are still just as high as ever, the barriers to effective competitive entry are almost non-existent. So what's a hard-working CEO supposed to do?

The simple answer is that you need to do it to yourself and do it to your business before your competitors do it to you. And the only way to stay in the game and pull this off is to keep raising the bar every chance you get. The world is divided into targets and gunslingers and, if you can't be a full-fledged gunslinger, then you'd better be a constantly moving target that's always a few steps ahead of the competition.

The test is "what's the best you can possibly be" and the answer is better (for the moment) than anyone else who's trying to do the same thing. And just because no one else has done something yet doesn't mean you shouldn't be aiming for it – you can't let other people's limitations hold you back. It's committing to a life of constant awareness (paranoia), continuous change and extreme flexibility as well as the willingness to eat and to abandon your "offspring" before they run out of steam. If you don't, you can be sure someone else will do it for you.

A good example of a great marketing company falling asleep at the switch is Nike. Simply stated, Nike owned the athlete for years. The coolest shoes, the coolest endorsements, the best technology and the coolest TV ads. When the Web came along, they put up a pretty robust website and made sure to show off their ads and their products and then - having fallen in love with their own videos - they just sat there resting on their laurels.

But the competitive race never waits for you. And, almost immediately, smart, fast competitors figured out that the real athletes weren't in it for the ads or the glory, they were in it for the blood, sweat and tears of the exercise and the sports. So a number of smart websites quickly emerged that served the real needs of the athletes – exercise programs, race training regimens, fitness tracking, socially connecting athletes with others who had like interests, athlete and team meet-ups, etc. – all aimed at providing real services and benefits to the athletes – not simply talking about it or trying to push products down their throats. But you can't win a race with your mouth.

And, in pretty short order, the real athletes (and plenty of weekend warriors as well) totally bailed on the Nike ad sites and moved over in the millions to these other service sites which were far more connected to their interests and far better uses of their scarce time. Nike blew it by not understanding that the expectations of customers are progressive – yesterday's novelties are today's old news. Nike failed to change their web offerings to meet the new needs and demands of their core customers and – as a result – opened the door for small, quick competitors to jump into the space with simple, straightforward tools and applications for runners and other athletes that permitted them to eat Nike's lunch.

Raising the bar means that you need to constantly outmode yourself and regularly cannibalize your products and services. It's not a linear or even an evolutionary process – it's utterly discontinuous and the fact is that what you're doing today may be meaningless tomorrow because the available technology takes a quantum leap and leaves your offerings in the dirt. The real test of Apple's relatively new CEO will be whether we see an iPhone 4S, iPhone 4X and an iPhone 4Z or we see a jump to the iPhone 5 that once again revolutionizes the marketplace.

The rate of change today is autocatalytic – each change creates the next change at a faster rate and leads to disruption and radical obsolescence – all driven by virality and almost perfect cross-market intelligence. If you want to stay in the game and run with the big dogs, keep raising the bar.

One last important thought – no one cares who made the first version of something – they only want to know who makes the best version.

YOU CAN'T ADD VALUE IF YOU DON'T HAVE VALUES

For new businesses, there are lots of things you just can't afford financially. Those things are typically (and painfully) pretty obvious. And I'm not just talking about fancy cars, frills, and bells and whistles. I'm talking about fairly basic, but sadly expensive, stuff. The good news, however, is that, as you grow your business, a lot of these kinds of problems will go away. I like to say that any problem that you can solve with a check isn't really a problem at all – it's just one of a million different choices you'll have to make as time goes on.

But there are a bunch of other things that start-ups also can't afford that have nothing to do with money. One of the most complicated and least talked about (in this feel-good, politically correct world we live in) is real values. You absolutely cannot afford to have the wrong values when you're building your business. In a word, you can't be pushing platitudes when you're trying to make payroll.

It makes me sick to read these retrospective (rewrite my life please) articles by people who've made it (sometimes thru hard work; sometimes thru luck; sometimes thru family ties or special connections; and sometimes for no apparent reason at all) talking about how important it was to their success that they had all these Mom & Pop, Apple Pie, and democratic (small "d") values as part of their businesses from the beginning. It's a complete crock. And what's worse is the fact that it can mislead other people into thinking that this is the way the real world works. But it's not.

As sad as it may sound and as bitter a pill as it may be to all the bleeding hearts and social scientists out there that have never run anything, the truth is that you need to adopt the values that are right for your business from time to time. As the joke goes, "These are my principles. If you don't like them, I have others.", but it's not really a joke. As a new company, you can't afford the luxury of having grown-up, fancy values when you are fighting for survival. And anyone who tells you otherwise just hasn't ever been there in the trenches looking right into the bottom or the wrong end of the barrel.

Now I'm not saying, of course, that you shouldn't have any concrete values, I'm just saying that the values that will make or break your business should and will change over time as your business and your team matures. This is actually a lot easier to show you than to try to describe. But first let me give you a few basics:

1. Your core values need to be manageable and realistic for your business.

2. Your core values need to be relevant to your business and your employees – not generic, but unique.

3. Your core values need to be short and memorable – the shorter the better – ideally they'd all fit on the back of your business card.

4. Your core values need to be as simple as possible, but no simpler.

5. Your core values need to be repeated constantly and internalized by everyone in the company.

At TFA, my college, our five core values are clear to all. We believe in:

> Unstinting Effort
> Pride of Craft
> Courage of Our Convictions
> Loyalty
> Excellence

Now, here are five core values from a large, mature corporation in our marketplace:

> Fairness
> Respect
> Opportunity
> Security
> Inclusion

I hope the differences are obvious. Not one of these words conveys any energy or a bias for action. They're pretty much entirely devoid of emotional content. And even if I knew what some of these words were intended to mean in the way of behavioral guidance, they don't tell me jack about what makes the company stand up and stand out every day. If you still don't get it, here's a visual aid:

Frankly, I couldn't build a fire under any group of employees with a stem-winder about inclusion or security if my life depended on it. In fact, in a start-up, attempts at too much inclusion are like ingesting a slow-acting poison that kills your response times, wastes enormous amounts of time and other resources, and almost always leads to mediocre results. I've said it before and I'll say it again – not every idea is a good idea – not every suggestion is worthy of extensive discussion - and democracy in meetings isn't really a virtue in and of itself. If I had the choice, I'd rather work for a tyrant any day than for a committee.

Again, there's nothing terribly wrong with these kinds of broad, vague values, they're just terribly wrong for a new, young business to try to live by or to live up to. And that's the real crux of the matter. You've got to make your core values real and you've got to make them matter or you're just wasting your breath. Company values don't break, they crumble slowly over time unless they are actively pursued and nurtured. It's a slippery slope and only you can stop the constant threat of erosion.

So, assuming you've got the right ones for your company's developmental stage and size, how do you protect and promote them? Three basic rules:

1. Make your company values aggressive and demanding

2. Make them inflexible and uncompromising

3. Be totally intolerant of breaches

Once your values start to slide, it's almost impossible to recover. And believe me nothing is more central to your company's culture and your ultimate shot at success than getting this process right. You're the values cop.

And nothing is harder because it's NEVER easy to say what no one wants to hear and it's the easiest thing in the world to give someone a temporary pass or to overlook something in the moment when you should jump on it. But remember two important things: (a) past sins never vanish, they just wait; and (b) you can't talk yourself out of problems that you behave yourself into. You've got to insist on the proper behaviors and the proper attitudes and stick to your guns.

It's your job – it's not fun; it's not easy – if it was, we'd all be making $12,500 a year – and it's a constant process that requires continual vigilance.

To make your core values stick, you've got to be prepared to take it to people every day and insist that they get on the program or go somewhere else. Don't confuse someone's good manners with their willingness to change their behavior – you need to make sure that their commitments aren't just words - and that their apologies aren't just lip service. Any apology not accompanied by a change in behavior is an insult.

SOMETIMES ENOUGH IS ENOUGH

I understand that nobody likes a quitter and that we all believe every captain should go down with his ship. These are among the few things in life today that everyone can agree on. But is this really a healthy attitude for the folks running a new business? Especially when they're spending other people's money at a ferocious clip? Sometimes you need to be smart enough to read the tea leaves and "quit when you're ahead" even if you're actually way behind and losing more ground every day. But how exactly do you ever know when enough is enough?

See - this is what's so tricky about clichés. We all grew up thinking that "quitting while you were ahead" meant grabbing your chips off the poker table and getting out of Dodge City (or Vegas as the case may be) with a pile of dough - even if your buddies tried to pull you back into the game and called you a sore winner for leaving <u>before</u> you started losing. Poker – as I'm sure you know – isn't really about making friends or being the most beloved guy at the table. It's about winning. Just like running a business.

And believe me, it's much tougher – personally and emotionally when the right time comes - to pull up stakes and shut down the business you've poured your heart and soul into than it is to piss off your poker pals over a few pesos. But it's part and parcel of the process - it comes with the job - and the final decision ultimately lands in your lap. So how can you figure out when the time is right?

There really isn't a simple answer or one solution for every situation, but there is a Rule that I have found to be useful in almost every case. I call it The Rule of 3 Ds and 3 Fs.

The 3 Ds are pretty simple. There are some things you've got to <u>D</u>O, to <u>D</u>ETERMINE and to <u>D</u>ISCUSS.

The main thing you've got to DO is to face the facts. If you can do this honestly, you'll be well on your way to the right conclusions about your particular situation. Because, while in good times denial is one of the greatest strengths of an entrepreneur, when things are moving in the wrong direction, you're simply can't afford to ignore them. And – at the end of the day – refusing to look at unpleasant facts and realities doesn't make them disappear or go away anyway. They don't vanish; they just wait and things in this life that don't get better only get worse.

People can have different opinions about the meaning of certain facts or circumstances and how to deal with them. It's funny that they'll call you persistent when you succeed and stubborn when you fail. But the facts always remain the same. They won't change by themselves and – once you do face them – you've got to have the courage and the wisdom to take the actions necessary to deal with them. In some cases, that means that you need to close the doors. And sometimes, as the leader, you need to help your team and your employees reach these same conclusions. You've got to give your people permission to make the hard calls and the tough decisions.

The next thing is to DETERMINE your true feelings about the situation. If you focus on your feelings and think about these statements, you'll have addressed the second F.

1. It's time to go when it's harder work to come to the office every day than any work you do once you get there.

2. It's time to go when you find yourself spending more time talking to yourself at the office than to anyone else.

3. It's time to go when you're constantly trying to do things cheaply that you shouldn't do at all because you can't afford to do them right.

4. It's time to go when you feel under-appreciated, taken advantage of, and let down by everyone else in the place.

5. It's time to go when you spend more time and energy at the office plotting your revenge than doing any meaningful or constructive work.

And let me just say on this score that, if you've actually ever run a business and you haven't experienced versions and degrees of all of these feelings, then you haven't really been an entrepreneur and you were most likely working for your folks.

The last task of the list is to DISCUSS your decision with your family and take their feelings into account. Family is the final F. Starting and running a business is just as tough – maybe tougher – on your family as it is on you. And because they aren't typically active in the business, it's even harder when things start to go south and they can't do much other than watch helplessly while you suffer. But here's the most important advice I can give you:

a. there's always more work and other businesses, but you've only got one family;
b. your family is a much more important extension and reflection of yourself than any work you do; and
c. your work is just that – it's your work and NOT who you are. It doesn't make or define you – it serves you and when it stops being valuable and additive for you <u>and</u> your family, it's time to do something else.

For better or worse – and because life isn't remotely fair - when things are really rotten and we have no place else to turn, sadly - we don't turn <u>to</u> our families, we turn <u>on</u> them and we take a lot of the crap out on them for no good reason other than that they're there. This is some of the most real and devastating damage that a failing business can cause and it's the most critical reason to get out when the time is right and not to prolong the agony.

It's like staying on the *Atkins* diet way too long. You don't lose any more weight – you're just much more miserable to be around every day. Life's too short and you spend too much of it working not to find and do something that you love and can be enthusiastic about every day. It's never too soon to stop living someone else's dream and make your own dreams come true.

Enough sometimes really is enough.

IT HELPS TO KNOW WHERE YOU'RE HEADED

There's an old adage about successful entrepreneurs which states that, if they knew how long and hard the start-up process was going to be, they wouldn't have set out on the journey in the first place. I think this may be true for a small fraction of entrepreneurs – mainly older career-changers who bail before they begin – but that it doesn't apply to the majority of the target group because (a) they're gluttons for punishment; (b) they basically wouldn't believe you even if you swore on two stacks of bibles; and – in any case – (c) they wouldn't listen to you (even if they thought you might be right) because their passion typically overwhelms their perspective as well as whatever objectivity they might still have. Bottom line – time, blood, sweat and tears - and a lot of hard work don't scare anyone who's really trying to make something important happen.

But what really kills any good entrepreneur is the fear of getting the short end of the stick in a negotiation and/or the feeling of being taken advantage of. These concerns are serious parts of every entrepreneur's mental make-up (when and whether they admit it is a different story) and they can lead to serious issues and problems down the line for all concerned. As often as not, they end up being the hardest problems to deal with when a business is about to be sold – the entrepreneur's somewhat naïve and long-standing expectations rarely match the realities of the situation. There's a simple reason for this recurring outcome and it starts very early in the investor/entrepreneur relationship. Very frankly, most young entrepreneurs don't spend anywhere near enough time doing the fundamental math that is crucial to answer the ultimate and very simple question – what am I going to end up with in <u>my</u> pocket when this deal is done? This isn't about being greedy or focusing too much on yourself – it's about setting reasonable metrics for success and aligning – to the greatest extent possible – the respective interests of the parties. If you spend some time early in the process addressing these kinds of issues, you can save yourself a lot of stress and some ugly surprises way down the line.

I've been working with several small teams of young guys with big plans and big ideas and a pretty clear and realistic view of what it's going to take to succeed. They're all fully prepared to climb any mountain, scale any wall, and honestly do whatever it takes to succeed from an effort and commitment standpoint. But they have only the vaguest idea of how to even think 3 to 5 years ahead and to try to calculate and understand the economics that will obtain at that time and which will really determine the value of their interests in the business. They need help in a hurry. But there's some good news. It's just not that complicated.

The very best negotiators go into battle (and these really are battles) with a range of expected outcomes. They may not always achieve the highest and best results, but at least they understand the various possibilities and they can prepare - mentally and emotionally- for them. Young entrepreneurs are so focused on the short run - get the money and get the business started - that they never sit down and really do the math. They don't spend the time to extend and envision the likely financial outcomes (given the required phases of funding and the time frames involved) and, as a result, they cut and/or accept deals way too often that doom them to end up at the end of the road with a bunch of nothing. They work their butts off; they get the funding they need; and they create jobs and a great company, but when they turn around and finally focus on their own finances, they discover that while they definitely bet the ranch, they personally ended up with a lot of other people's gratitude and a pocket full of rocks. That's not how the world is supposed to work, but that's the hard truth in too many cases.

And here's another little piece of bullshit that needs to be put to bed. No one else is gonna do it for you. When it comes to bucks, you gotta look out for your own bacon. No boards of directors will do it for you. Your buddies have their own agendas and their family's mouths to feed. And you'd be surprised at how little time these days supposedly astute investors (who've typically never run anything) spend worrying about the management's compensation and incentives of the people running their portfolio companies. When everyone in the world wants to be an entrepreneur, you could almost forgive these guys (although I never would) for being arrogant enough to think that even the best founders and CEOs are just cogs in the big wheel of business - readily replaced, grateful to be in the game, and a dime a dozen. And while their facts aren't necessarily wrong, their philosophy in this regard is short-sighted and stupid and just results in a lot of angry and unhappy people.

So, as someone sitting across the table from a team of smart, seasoned scumbags (sorry - did I really say that?), how do you - the relative novice - try to develop a strategy, a rationale, and an attitude (at least as important to the process) to carry you successfully through the multiple series of negotiations that you'll be part of as you build (and fund) your business. You need to build a roadmap in reverse. It's not that hard, but it's absolutely essential to securing the right results for you. It may not always work, but if it's rational and realistic, it's at least a working framework and a hook to hang your hat on. Keep in mind that in reality no one knows anything for sure about this process. There are no "one size fits all" rules. There's no gospel or black letter law - every deal is different, every deal is personal, and every deal depends on the parties and their relative degrees of preparation, passion, and patience. In the land of the blind, the guy with the reverse roadmap wins.

So what exactly is a reverse roadmap? Think of it as a rigorous exercise in developing a realistic analysis, a set of often reduced expectations, and a target set of rational (ideally achievable) results. And the rule of thumb for doing this couldn't be simpler - if you know where you want to end up and you've developed several reasonable routes to get there, you're just that much more likely to avoid detours, distractions, and nasty dilution and to reach your goal. On the other hand, if you're so head-down and focused on funding the day-to-day and fighting the fires and you don't take time to focus at least a little on your future (even though I know there's no hurry 'cause you're gonna live forever), you're not going to be that happy when the dust finally settles and you discover, from a financial perspective, that the whole painful struggle looks in retrospect like you spent your precious time kissing your sister instead of stepping out with Shakira or jet setting with J Lo. But it doesn't have to end up that way.

Now keep in mind that I'm not talking about your business plan. I know that you've got a business plan. And I'm sure you've also got a pile of financial projections for your operations in every size and shape. I'm talking about a fiscal projection for your future pocketbook. A tiny little cheat sheet that keeps you on track which you can keep in your wallet, paste on your forehead, or write down on the back of your business card (if you still use one). The numbers may change over time and need to be updated to reflect new facts and circumstances, but this little tool will help keep you focused when it matters on the ultimate goal line. And because you have a "plan", every conversation you have on the subject is clearer and convincing because we all know the guys on the other side are just winging it - or worse - making it up as they go.

What you need to succeed is just a piece of paper with a few columns (3) and a few rows (4 for each round of expected financing) on it. It might help to have 2 or 3 basic business metrics on the page as well, but it's not critical because this exercise is all about funding. Here is the entire matrix:

<u>Year One</u>　　　　　　<u>Year Two</u>　　　　　　<u>Year Three</u>

BUSINESS METRICS
- Revenues
- Headcount

CURRENT ROUND
- Financial Investor
- Strategic Investors
- Post-$ Val
- MGMT Stake (%)
- MGMT Value ($)

NEXT ROUND (Date)
- Follow-On Invsrs
- New Invsrs
- Post-$ Val
- MGMT Stake (%)
- MGMT Value ($)

THIRD ROUND (Date)
- Follow-ON Investors
- New Invstrs
- Post-$ Val
- MGMT Stake (%)
- MGMT Value ($)

Don't have all the answers at your fingertips? Not to worry – no one else does either. But start the exercise and slowly you'll develop some level of comfort with the process and put up some real numbers on the board. Some may be wishful thinking – but the way I see it is that wishful thinking beats not thinking about and planning for these things by a mile. Remember, in basketball, it's "nothin' but net", but in business, it's ultimately all about "net worth". You can't let your passion warp your long-term perspective because you don't get that many great bites at the apple and you need to make each one count especially when you're riding a winner. Winning takes some getting used to and a lot of hard work, but it's the name of the game.

HOW TO TALK YOURSELF OUT OF A JOB

It's time to bring back *The Peter Principle*. Not the BBC TV series, but the idea that meritocracies work to eventually promote people beyond the level of their actual abilities. And this time, it's not as a management concept about premature or inappropriate promotion – it's as a warning to everyone under 30 who are not grateful for the jobs they have and who want more – especially too much more too soon. If ever there was a time to be really careful about what you wish for, it would be right now.

So what's *The Peter Principle* anyway? Of course you can *Google* it, but *Wikipedia* is much faster and easier. The simplest phrasing is that "employees tend to rise to their level of incompetence." It was initially a humorous formulation until people started to see how accurate a description it turned out to be. But no one really talks about it anymore today although it's far more prevalent than ever in our government; our military; and especially in our schools.

And, if you're young and not careful, it's a quick way to lose your job. In fact, I just had to sit through a very painful and embarrassing meeting where a perfectly decent and talented young man was unsuccessfully asking for his old job back. But his old job had been filled. And basically, because he had vocally and aggressively sought the new job that he really wasn't right for; he had essentially "hoisted himself on his own petard". This one you'll want to definitely *Google* which will take you straight to *Wikipedia*.

Young people today seem to understand only half of the phrase "up or out", but it's a fact of life. I encourage everyone to aspire to greater things and to take their best shot – but only (a) when they are prepared; (b) when they understand what they're asking for; and (c) when they're prepared to live with the consequences of things not working out.

So don't be in such a hurry that you leap before you look. Before you jump for that new job; you just might want to honestly answer these questions for yourself.

1. Make Sure You Understand What the *Whole* New Job Entails

If you just focus on the perks and the apparent rewards of a job, you often miss the whole package and especially the baggage that comes with the benefits. Especially in sales, there's a whole lot of ugly lifting that goes with getting the job done. I had a client once who won some hugely profitable government contracts and it seemed like a piece of cake. Then I spent a week on the road with him going from one Army base to another entertaining procurement people in cheap, smoky bars for hours on end and dealing with a stream of insufferable self-important assholes and I decided that life was way too short for that shit and you couldn't pay me enough to put up with it for a second. He knew it too, but it was a choice he had made and it came with the job.

2. Make Sure You Can Do the Job

Hope and wishful thinking aren't good tools for advancement. I suppose that in our dreams we all think that we can do anything, but in the real world our "can do's" have to keep up with our "want to's" or we end up in deep doo doo. This is where honest assessment (and maybe even asking some other people whose opinion and judgment you respect) comes into play. The very last thing you want to do is to test the depth of the pool with both feet – it's a great way to end up all wet - even assuming that you don't drown. As they say in the South: "if wishes were Porsches, poor boys would drive".

3. Make Sure You Really Want the Job

The grass is almost always greener. It's like guys watching TV – they know what's on – but they <u>want</u> to know what <u>else</u> is on. Travel and time out of the office sounds great until you miss the first few family occasions, a few school recitals, and spend a few too many rancid nights in the *Red Roof Inn*. Other jobs are so stressful and so 24/7 that the sacrifices they entail (family, friends, etc.) simply aren't worth it in the long run. There's always more work – you've only got one family.

In addition, some jobs look easy from the outside and some may actually just be easy. But you'll find that the hardest work is actually to do nothing or next to nothing. And here's the truth – real happiness doesn't come from doing easy work or just phoning it in. It comes from doing hard work really well. If you don't put the effort into something, you never really know and appreciate what it's worth. And remember that your work and how you feel about it has a lot to do with your sense of self – if you'd rather be doing anything but your work; find something else to do.

4. Make Sure It's a Real Job that Matters

Sometimes, the easiest way to get someone to shut up and get them out of your hair is to say "yes". You want to be sure that you're not ending up with a make-work job and some lip service that your boss created just to stop the constant chatter. You need to make sure what you're doing matters. Otherwise, you might as well be Dolly Parton's feet. It's great to throw yourself into things and work hard at something, but you want to work hard at something that's worth doing.

In addition, in today's economy, you've got to look at each job through two distinct lenses. Does it have meaning? Does it have value? If no one values or cares about the results of your efforts, it may be meaningful to you, but does it really matter to the business or your bosses? If not, it won't be around for long. In the book and newspaper business, and a world of user-generated crap, I think that real editors must ask themselves these kinds of questions every day and I bet that they don't like the answers.

5. Make Sure You Know Who You'll Be Working With

Some people you may get stuck working with (above or below you) can turn the best job in the world into a miserable experience. I'd rather work with tree stumps than some of the people I've had to deal with over the years. I think that some people are only alive today because it's against the law to kill them. Try not to end up working with or for them. And while you're at it – try not to work for someone who has more problems than you do.

6. Make Sure that Management is Committed

It's not easy to look a gift horse in the mouth – especially one that you begged for, but you need to make sure before you sign up that management and the company will provide what you need to succeed: funding and other resources; authority to get things done; enough time and runway; and, most importantly, some agreed-upon metrics for what will constitute success. Without the proper tools, time, and a measurable set of objectives and goals; you'll be chasing your tail in no time.

7. Make Sure that You not Getting Just Enough Rope to Hang Yourself

I don't want to be too cynical, but here's another fact of life: it's a lot harder to have to flat out fire someone (especially someone you'd like to keep, but can't afford) than it is to let them work themselves out of a "new" job that just doesn't end up working out. Believe me, it happens more than you'd imagine.

So, here's the bottom line: do your homework before you open your mouth and ask for that new position. It will save you a lot of heartache and maybe your current job as well. Sometimes not getting what you think you desperately want is the best break of all.

WHY RABBITS DON'T RUN BIG BUSINESSES

I've always been partial to Thumper's Dad's advice about communication. In case you don't recall it from the *Bambi* movie, his Dad said: "If you can't say something nice, don't say nothin' at all" - at least as Thumper recalled it. And, as it happens, this is pretty good advice for small talking animals, but it's a really bad way to run your company. You can't build a successful business based on a culture that values quiet, courtesy and consensus over honest conversations, constructive criticism and confrontations where necessary. Politely keeping the peace can't ever trump telling the truth. The best operators know two things for certain: (1) the truth only hurts when you don't tell it and (2) the truth only hurts when it should. I realize that sometimes it's very hard to tell the truth, but it's just as hard to hide it and a whole lot less productive.

White lies and other pleasantries are worthless – they're a lot like eating junk food – you get a temporary lift, but no nourishment; the problem persists; the emptiness returns; and nothing gets done in the meantime. And when you encourage people to lie even a little, you learn quickly that people who will lie for you will eventually lie to you. Better a few bruises and battered egos than a bankrupt business based on bullshitting each other. And honestly, it's just so much easier for everyone because when you always tell the truth, you never have to waste time and energy trying to remember your lies.

Frankly, an aggressive culture where people stand their ground and argue their cases makes for much better ultimate decisions as long as people are arguing for the right reasons. The right reasons are to get to the truth and the best results for the business and not because people need to be right and won't shut up until they grind everyone down and wear everyone else out. Make your point; say your piece; and sit your butt down. Don't argue with the truth.

You want your people to fearlessly face the facts. As one of the great old Hollywood moguls used to say: "I want my people to tell me the truth even if it costs them their jobs". But seriously, unpleasant facts don't fade away when you ignore them – they fester – and refusing to look at them won't change the situation or improve things until you do something about them. Facts may change, but the truth never does. And waiting only makes things worse. It's a funny thing about the truth – the truth doesn't have a time of its own. There's never a better or best time to tell someone the truth – the time for truth is always <u>now</u>.

I think all of the foregoing comes down to a few simple "rules" which you need to share (somewhat obsessively) with all of your people (not just newbies in orientations) on a regular and recurring basis. My suggested and very basic rules are as follows:

1. <u>Tell the Truth</u>

No shades, no strokes, no "smoothing" the news or softening the blows – give it to me simple and straight. Figures don't lie, but they often don't tell the whole story. Make sure that the metrics don't get in the way of a clear message. As they say, everyone is entitled to their own opinion, but the facts are the facts – you don't get to pick and choose them.

2. Tell It Timely

Nothing ugly really improves over time. Don't wait to bring me bad news. The sooner and shorter the better. I need a brief, not as book. Nothing elaborate – just accurate information delivered on time and in time.

3. Tell Everyone

Don't assume that everyone else (or anyone else) necessarily knows what you know. Spread the word. In addition to the general virtues of transparency and making sure that eventually the message does get thru to the right people; going wide makes it more likely that meaningful and actionable information will also get to people who need whether you even realize that or not.

4. Tell It 'til Someone Listens

I don't think that, in most businesses, you can <u>ever</u> over-communicate relevant and time-sensitive data. But you will often encounter people who fall into two problem piles: (a) people who don't want to say what nobody wants to hear; and (b) people who don't want to hear what needs to and has to be said and spread throughout the organization. These folks are master manipulators and they typically follow the standard three-step routine in dealing with "inconvenient", but sadly true facts: (i) first they aggressively ridicule; (ii) then they violently resist; and finally (iii) they get with the program – claim that they knew it all along – and treat things as obvious and self-evident. You need to keep spreading the word until you're sure that you've done as much as you can reasonably do to let the folks in charge know what you know. If they don't listen after that, so be it. It's frustrating and depressing, but in many businesses, it's a fact of life. As Bruce Springsteen says: "When the truth is spoken and it makes no difference – something in your heart goes cold". After a while, if it's clear that you're wasting your breath, find a better place to be.

5. Tell It All the Time

And finally, truth-telling is not a sometime thing. As with everything else that matters in your business, it's an everyday, all day part of creating and maintaining an environment where the organization learns and grows and where things continue to improve through a constant iterative process. You can't make innovation through iteration work if you don't have a constant and accurate flow of data telling you what's working and what's not and where you're going wrong.

NETWORKING TIPS FROM THE TOP

Last week I had the privilege of sitting on a panel with two extremely successful serial entrepreneurs (Sam Yagan – founder of *OkCupid* and now CEO of *Match.com* and Chuck Templeton – founder of *Open Table* and now MD of the ImpactEngine accelerator at 1871) which was moderated by my good friend, Rob Wolcott, who runs the Kellogg Innovation Network (KIN). The title of the panel was slightly longer than the typical length of my blog posts (so I don't want to repeat it here) and no good entrepreneur stays on point anyway - so let's just say that it was an evening of quips and networking tips from a bunch of very smart and experienced people. I learned and laughed a lot (and caught a few things that were new ideas to me as well) and I thought I'd share a couple of the highlights.

1. Walk the Walk and Wear the T-Shirt

I'm usually the most under-dressed guy at grown-up events like this, but Sam Yagan was wearing a *Match.com* t-shirt under his jacket so, from a sartorial splendor standpoint, it was pretty much a draw. The more important point was what Sam said about why he was wearing the shirt and what wearing the shirt says about Sam. He said that, as the CEO, he's always selling and promoting the business and that it's a critical part of that process that everyone he meets knows that he's all-in, fully-committed, and sincerely does believe that Match.com will change your life for the better and, if you've got the time, he'll tell you how and why.

My friend Slava Rubin who co-founded *Indiegogo* (and is now the CEO) always wears a company t-shirt when he travels. He's plenty proud of the business he's built too and it shows the minute you meet him and you'll miss your plane for sure if he gets started talking about the company and the latest and greatest crowd funding successes that they've helped to make happen. He says, of course, that his shirt's a comfy way to roll, but the real reason is that he knows he's going to pass a bunch of people on the trip and it's the cheapest form of subliminal advertising he's come up with so far which also saves him a bundle on marketing.

It's all about authenticity, believing in your business and yourself and walking the walk. Leaders lead by example or they don't really lead at all. The day you're not comfortable in your role, in the business, or in the company t-shirt, is the day you should find another place to be. If you're not excited about what you're doing and proud of the place you doing it, do something else. This stuff (building new businesses and changing the world) is just too hard and life's too short to go to work every day without a spring in your step and a smile on your face. Not everything will ever be fun and easy, but as long as it matters and you're making a difference, there's no better place to be.

2. You Never Know Who's Going to Bring You Your Future

Rob Wolcott likes to say that at KIN he tries to never leave serendipity to chance, but Chuck Templeton told the audience two different ways that – in the early days of his business - he manufactured and mined his own serendipity. One was a process and one was an attitude and they both helped him build his earliest networks of supporters and sponsors and also

– crucially – helped him fill in the gaps in his knowledge and experience by reaching out to others for help.

The process was pretty simple. He'd read every issue of what - for a few minutes back then - was more or less the hot tech industry magazine (**The Industry Standard**) – which he described as an early version of **WIRED** (although the fact is that **WIRED** was started about 5 years before it) and when he read about people doing things that seemed interesting and relevant to his business, he would reach out to them and ask them for a few minutes of their time to answer his questions. Not only did he learn a lot about stuff, but he said that he also learned a lot about how many people were so generous with their time and how they would actually take the time to help a total stranger. The moral of the story was pretty simple – it never hurts to ask – and it can often turn into a real opportunity and it's always an education.

The attitude was also pretty straightforward. He said that you should always keep an open mind when you meet people and that you should never underestimate them because you really just never know who's going to turn out to have the keys to the kingdom. Or as I like to say: you never know who's going to bring you your future. Every encounter, every meeting, every conversation is a chance to learn and also to build and extend your network. Everyone's an example – some to emulate and some to avoid like the plague – but you'll never know which ones are which if you don't invest the time to explore the possibilities and have the right attitude while you're at it.

SNAPCHAT – SAYING IT DOESN'T MAKE IT SO

I wrote recently about my concern that too many young entrepreneurs had what I called "situational ethics" and that they believed that it was "nice" to tell the truth (or the whole truth) when it was quick or convenient, but that it certainly wasn't essential – especially when it got in the way of getting something else done. A little inaccuracy can save a ton of explanation – if you don't care about your reputation or your customers.

Sadly, too many of these characters don't really care about anything but themselves. Certainly they have no time or truck for things as vague as honesty and some kind of basic business morality. It's like they were raised in a values vacuum. These are my values, but if you don't like them or they don't suit, I've got others as well. Something to fit every occasion.

Then – when the truth gets out and they've got to explain to millions of ripped-off and disappointed users - they go for cheap excuses and try to paper over the problem with legalese and after-the-fact improvements to their boilerplate policies and written disclosures. Worse yet, I see too many cases where there's an even more upsetting and gratuitous attitude toward their customers (who, after all, are millions and millions of young kids with their own "whatever" attitudes) – they not only take them for granted; they take them for idiots who just really don't care about these things or wilful co-conspirators who are just as likely to forget and forgive a little "mistake" here or there in the service of the greater good – making a lot of money and sticking it to the man. After all, what your parents can't see or share, they can't bust your chops about what you're not supposed to be doing once they do. Snapchat and sexting *uber alles*.

And now, we have the two Snapchat co-creators who have stepped up to be the poster boys for flagrant fiction followed – once they've been caught red-handed in their lies – by slick and superficial attempts to say they're sorry. Saying you're sorry doesn't mean a thing unless you mean it and it isn't worth a thing if what you're sorry about is getting caught – not screwing up in the first place.

Their mediocre and self-serving mea culpa blog post is a complete crock. "We were so busy building" that we didn't pay "enough" attention to the very things that were the core principles and the basic value proposition of our product – privacy and ephemerality. It turns out that the government has determined that (a) the "snaps" don't necessarily disappear in a few seconds; (b) that Snapchat's claims and promises about privacy were lies; (c) that the alert notification system was also flawed and by-passable; and (d) that private location and other data were being collected even though Snapchat expressly said that this was not happening.

The fact that they've settled their "dispute" with the FTC's division of privacy and identity protection where they were accused of deceiving their users and multiple misrepresentations to consumers about how things actually worked and with whom they've now agreed to hire an independent expert watchdog for the next 20 years doesn't mean squat and certainly doesn't give me any confidence that anyone has learned anything useful from this episode. I'm just hoping against hope that the tens of millions of people who have been duped decide that maybe there's another product or service that does the same job (maybe even a better job) and that it's a smarter tool and place to do the stupid things that they want to do.

But all of this noise isn't really the lesson for smart entrepreneurs who are trying to create real businesses and real value for themselves, their users and their investors. The point is much simpler – it's just too easy today to build something that looks good and seems to solve a problem or create a solution on the surface – this is the triumph of form over substance – but, if you're in such a big hurry to get something out there in the market and you don't take the time and invest the hard work and the necessary resources to build the infrastructure necessary to really deliver on your promises into your product or services at the beginning, then ultimately you haven't built anything real or lasting. Your solution won't scale. Your design won't survive real due diligence. Your prospective acquirers will be happy to take the concept, but not the code or the crew. And you'll find out that you built a toy – not a technology and wasted a lot of time in the process.

The biggest shame in the Snapchat story is not that they were unethical egotists; it's that they were bad engineers.

DO MY STEPS COUNT IF MY FITBIT ISN'T COUNTING THEM?

While I'm sure that philosophers for many years to come (if they're still around) will continue to wrestle with the question of whether a tree falling in the forest makes a sound if there's no one there to hear it; today's pressing dilemmas are more social and digital in nature. Whether we like it or not, while that tree may still be all alone in the forest, we're almost never actually alone these days and the advent of constant connectivity and two-way datafication is changing the ways in which we behave in surprising and unexpected ways.

We're connected to our friends and family, our co-workers and employers, a multitude of info-grabbing apps, and frankly a whole host of other folks, businesses, and agencies that we hardly know or know much about. And because our "phones" – actually I'd call them digital trackers that happen to make phone calls – are transmitting our thoughts, actions, locations and activities – actively and passively – knowingly and not – all day long, the communication and surveillance loop is persistent, omnipresent and unending.

It's like we have a digital Jiminy Cricket strapped to our waists instead of sitting on our shoulder – but the end result is virtually the same. Your tracker may not be offering moral support (or judgments), but it's tracking your movements all the same and sharing those with the world. And, as we all know from Professor Heisenberg's uncertainty principle, we behave differently when we know we're being watched (and/or measured) and this is why we like to say that "what gets measured is what gets done".

Now, if all this surveillance and digital peer pressure results in more exercise or other positive activities and actions, I suppose that's a good thing. But there is definitely such a thing as too much of a good thing and I'm thinking we're getting pretty close to the tipping point. And you may think that you're immune from these kinds of influences (and for the moment that may be true), but it's only a matter of time (and which poison you pick) because, in the end, they're gonna get us all and most of us will come along willingly.

As our technologies become more and more mobile and miniaturized (and – at least for now – wholly dependent on the life of our batteries), it appears that the power of constant connectivity may be at least as enslaving and annoying as it is theoretically empowering. And, just as an aside, is it too damn much to ask the phone manufacturers to have a phone whose battery lasts at least through a reasonably long business day? I love the new kinetic battery guys (like MyPowr.me), but do we really need to be carrying yet another device with us just to have enough juice to make it home at night?

In any case, I'm not just talking here about dedicated/obsessive users of any stripe: email junkies, crackberry addicts, selfie sickies, or even Google glassholes – I'm talking about anyone wearing a Fitbit, Jawbone, heart-monitoring watch or any other gizmo that charts and communicates athletic, calorie-burning or other aspects of your activity. The fact is that these powerful little guys strapped to our waists can be constructive coaxers or demanding dictators. We're seeing new (non-chemical) kinds of addictions – manufactured right before our eyes – in fact manufactured by us for us

- which are built on datafication systems driven in large part by peer and partner pressure. These programs are beginning to change our behaviors at scale. And it's equally clear that there are psychological changes which are accompanying the introduction and adoption of these kinds of systems.

If you don't believe that this is a problem here and now, just see how you react when you discover midday that you forgot to sufficiently charge your device and it's no longer measuring your activity. We've all already experienced the angst associated with our mobile phones dying, but this is even worse. And, if you really want to go "cold turkey", just see how hard it is to put your device on the bed stand one morning and try to "leave home without it". I don't think you can do it.

Why is this so important for all of us and especially for the next several generations? It's not because I really care whether you're a few steps ahead or behind me in tonight's rankings or that your place on the leader board is far above mine. These are just the measurements and outcomes of the disease. The disease is that our technology now connects us and lets us work as long and hard as we want. All the time if we like.

The seductive power of constant and ubiquitous connectivity is that we don't want to turn it off. We don't want to drop out or disconnect. But if each of us doesn't start to think about limits and boundaries and rules, there won't be any end to anyone's day or anything meaningful left in our lives outside of work. The Fitbit anxiety is just the "canary in the coalmine" and an early symptom of the bigger problem. And the bottom line for each and every one of us in the most personal terms is very simple.

There's always more work, but you've only got one family and one time to go around this crazy life. So I'd say that now's the time to start thinking about how to balance all of the things that are really important in making a life (and not just in making a living) and try to get some sense of balance and proportion back in your life before it's too late.

BE THE ONE THEY CAN COUNT ON

It's not just Country Music that we rely on to say the simple things that need sayin'. And the Blues don't have any monopoly on tellin' it like it is (or how it ain't) or the way it should be. The fact is that, over the years, many songs from other genres have also told some basic stories which then resonated with millions of listeners and turned those "hits" into timeless classics. The format was inexpensive and the songs were "popular"; but that said nothing about the depth and reality of the feelings they successfully evoked. Even big boys do occasionally cry - as does everyone else. Music moves us all to extremes.

Sometimes, but only rarely, the elements that drove the widespread appreciation of these special tunes were the song's memorable hook; a special intro (like Keith's on *Satisfaction*); or a guitar solo (think Carlos Santana) that seemed permanently stuck in our minds. Most of the time, however, it was the immediate and intimate connection that we had with the lyrics which sealed the deal. They seemed to be speaking directly to us and "killing us softly" with a sensation of unexpected emotion. They surprised and touched us because they spoke to and about the very things that were important in our own lives. The truth is that music and music alone has both the power <u>and</u> our permission to enter our lives every day and excite and move us in these magical ways. As Sara Bareilles says in *Brave*: music can turn a phrase into a weapon or a drug.

But putting all the "love" (including love of country) and all the "loss" songs aside, what strikes me is that the singly most successful and consistent message in the largest number of classic songs (which are as powerful and telling today as they were on the day they were written and first performed) is one that's just as significant in our business lives as it is in our personal affairs. It's about the importance of being there.

Think about it.

What have you got "when you're down and troubled and you need a helping hand"? Of course, you've got a friend.

And who will "take your part when darkness comes and pain is all around"? Simon and Garfunkel - for sure.

And for all those times "in our lives when we all have pain - we all have sorrow"? We know we can lean on … Bill Withers.

Everyone needs someone in their lives that they can count on – someone to call when there's no one else to call. And, these days, with radical change and ongoing disruption being a constant part of every business, the most valuable people in any company are the ones you can count on in a crisis or a crunch – the "go-to" guys and girls. The people who are there in a pinch and who you just naturally tend to run <u>to</u> – not <u>from</u> – when the feces hit the fan.

This isn't part of anyone's job description. And it's not something you can create on the fly or on the spot. It's a visceral feeling that you just get about the people who've got it. But here's the good news. It's something you can build over time (like any other part of your reputation) and it's something that you can work on and work at every day that you're at work and – over time – if you're truly committed and your efforts are sincere and authentic; you can make it happen.

And, just in case it's not obvious, there's no better investment you could possibly make in your career or your future than being the <u>first</u> stop when someone's looking for help and not the <u>last</u> resort.

So what does it take to get it done?

1. <u>Stay Up (Perspiration)</u>

Be the early bird at the office. Effort and energy trump talent all day long. And it never hurts to be the night owl too. Not the guy who's the last to leave the office TGIF party, but the person who puts in the extra time to make sure that things are done right the first time. Turns out that the buddies you buy beers for aren't very often the ones you'd bet your business on. And, as often as not, while you're bellying up to the bar (or buying someone a breakfast burrito the next morning); the real winners are back at the ranch taking care of business.

2. <u>Step Up (Passion)</u>

Make sure that everyone knows you're interested and available. That you're excited about the business and the opportunities and that you really want to be a part of the program. Ya gotta want it and it's gotta show. You need to put it out there and understand that all anyone can do is say "no" – they won't eat you. And – if you keep asking – I guarantee you that it'll only be a "no for now" and it'll be full speed ahead soon enough. You won't get your shot if you don't take every opportunity to try and you'll miss 100% of the shots you don't take. Anyone who tells you it's not cool to be out front and eager these days will soon be changing the bottles on the water cooler while you're being welcomed into the club.

3. Study Up (Preparation)

Even in the world of great entrepreneurial BS-ers, it actually does help to know what you're talking about. "Wingin' it" is good for sports bars and on Thanksgiving, but it's not a strategy for success in business. As I said recently, saying you don't know something these days isn't a commentary on your lack of knowledge – it's a confession of laziness and lack of interest – because the information is out there today; it's mostly a matter of looking. And if you cared; you'd care enough to get the answers before the questions were asked. The kind of knowledge, research and situational awareness that matter don't grow on trees or happen automatically or without help. You've got to put in the time, do the looking, and ask for assistance (when you don't have or can't find all the answers) in order to be ready when someone asks you for a hand.

4. Stand Up (Principles)

You can't create value if you don't have a set of real values of your own that consistently guide and inform the way you behave. Charismatic leaders can attract a lot of followers, but the attraction is to themselves rather than to something greater and more important. Cause leaders bring the multitudes along with them in support of doing things that matter and make a difference not simply to a single business, but in terms of a broader and more general good. It's important for the people you work with (and for) to understand that – while we don't expect anyone, but a monk to be utterly selfless – you believe that the best plans and the best businesses are focused on creating situations where everyone can be benefitted and where it's a win-win-win all around. Not easy to engineer or to pull off, but very important in the end.

5. Stick to It (Perseverance)

Execution is everything. Keeping at it – getting knocked down and picking yourself up again – making it clear that you won't settle for less or take "no" for an answer — these are all behaviors and traits that give off a certain vibration that the big dogs in the business will quickly sense and pick right up on because (a) it's absolutely a part of their own DNA and (b) it's also a big part of what got them to where they are. Winners have a Spidey-sense about other winners and, while their ears don't exactly perk up like a dog's; you can't miss the shift in their interest and attention when they encounter another of their own species. Wanting to win is fine — wanting to do the work that it takes to win and to keep at it until you do win is what makes the difference in the end.

That's all it takes. You can make it happen and there's no time like the present to get started. It's a lifelong iterative journey and the good news is that it gets better all the time.

If there's a goal or an endpoint to the process, it's very simple. When the chips are down and the fat's in the fire, you want to be the one who people can count on.

A/B TESTING IS SO YESTERDAY - AND SO'S YOUR MBA

The New York Times recently ran a piece on how the traditional and lengthy MBA programs were under growing pressure because – in addition to questions about the actual economic value of such costly offerings - their emphasis on corporate finance and strategy was increasingly being seen as irrelevant to the skill sets required in today's competitive marketplace where success is largely driven by speed, constant iteration, and the rapid abandonment of bad ideas. See N.Y. Times article here: http://www.nytimes.com/2014/12/26/business/mba-programs-start-to-follow-silicon-valley-into-the-data-age.html?ref=technology&_r=0 .

As hard as it may be to believe, it's possible that, in the next few years, the stigma attached to the MBA may even increase. If that happens, I'd say it was no big deal or any great loss because it's been years in coming; it's well-deserved; and it all began when the top schools became more concerned (if not obsessed) with inflating their annual rankings in a single magazine (*U.S. News & World Report*) than with the rigor and relevance of their courses. In cultures where punctuality is more valued than productivity; where there are no rewards for risk takers; and where maintaining the peace is more important than making progress – what else would you expect?

But what really bothered me in the article was the description of the ongoing, frantic, and utterly expected and lemming-like responses of the business schools to the problem. The author said that they were going to "follow Silicon Valley into the Data Age" by adopting the best practices they saw in the outside world and adding courses in stats, data science and A/B testing. Focusing on A/B testing – as if it's the new tool in town - when the rest of the world (powered by high-velocity, real-time computing and a flood of data drawn instantly from the marketplace) is simultaneously testing and evaluating variables ranging from A to Z is like trying to get the very best price you can on a great new VCR. Or building a new buggy whip.

It's so backward and embarrassing that it's almost hard to believe. The only thing more frightening than this kind of technical ignorance in action is the idea that some of our best and brightest students at these schools are being subjected to out-of-date and hidebound academics making bad, group-think decisions which are very much akin to the tech-blind leading the oblivious.

Trying to create market-responsive and timely training solutions without really understanding what massive changes are going on in the marketplace and what new decision-making tools and other resources have been created by the rapid expansion and deployment of new, low-cost and ubiquitous technologies; the growth of market and transactional transparency and measurement; and the impact of constant connectivity to the consumer – whenever and wherever – is like working in the dark or in the Dark Ages. It's not that MBA students aren't being trained in the use of data to make better informed decisions – it's that they are being trained by faculty members who are so far behind the times that they don't even know what kind of data now exists or the power of that data to be applied in new ways to predict and change behaviors in real time.

Matters of education around data and technology which are this important to our country's economy are probably too important to be left to educators. The right solutions and our future progress are going to be dictated and changed by active disruptors with unique and original ideas that are far more likely to be based in their visions (and even their dreams) than in their own practical experience or prior education. The changes required are discontinuous leaps forward and not linear extensions of legacy systems and programs. In many ways, it's as if the world is finally waking up to the fact that our existing educational institutions just don't have the tools or the chops to get the job done any more. These schools are selling their students what they have to sell and not what it takes today to succeed.

And just to be clear, so also are you in your own business. We all get stuck in these ruts after a while in any business and – as we start out the New Year – we can all learn how to pull ourselves out of the mud if we look closely at the 3 basic reasons that cause the problem. Because remember, if you only do what you've always done; you'll only get what you've always got - or a lot less – becd.

As I see it, there are basically three reasons why we (and so many of our institutions) so often end up in such a sorry place where we're going sideways at best and – more likely – slipping backwards.

First, we need to understand and acknowledge that the way we have conventionally done things to date is neither inevitable nor the only or best way to accomplish the results we are seeking. In addition, the results we are getting from our efforts today aren't the ultimate results or the maximum amounts we can achieve – they're just what we can do now. These aren't limits dictated by the inherent conditions or the available resources – they are limits determined by our present lack of vision as to what is possible and will be possible as our tools and technologies continue to improve. If we accept the current state as our limits, we limit our ability to grow beyond them. If we only see what we are looking for and we accept that as a boundary, we'll be left behind by those whose vision exceeds their grasp and who are hell-bent on continuing to grow until that is no longer the case.

Second, when we talk about the future, we need to develop a new language and vocabulary because – at the moment – our ability to share and explain our dreams and visions is bound up and limited by the words and phrases we have at hand. In the context of the business schools, when you are completely surrounded and consumed by the day-to-day operations and the commonplace, there's very little prospect that you can successfully look outside of yourself and your surroundings to see what's really going on. It's like trying to explain the ocean to a fish who's lived in that environment all its life. What you've always taken for granted, you lose the ability to change. Large educational institutions are completely reliant on predictability and linearity – they need the trains to run on time – and they hate surprises. But in the real world surprises and the joy of discovery mean everything and they are the very stuff of change. And this is why it's so sad to see discussions about moving from A to B when the real opportunities are to think about moving from A to infinity and beyond.

Third, we need to steal yet another important idea from nature. Goalless planning and progress. In nature, evolution doesn't proceed toward some known, defined or even arbitrary goal. The movement is not <u>toward</u> anything; it is movement away from constraints. Everything in nature wants to be free and unlimited. The goal is never to grow to a certain place or size – it's to never stop growing in every possible direction. And nature offers neither rewards for growth nor punishments – there are only consequences.

As we look to the future, we also need to adopt the same type of methodology for goalless planning – we need to keep moving forward and measuring our progress – but without accepting the idea that there is <u>only</u> a defined and known goal in mind. This is too minor and petty a vision to permit us to leap forward. The very nature of the future is one of moving targets and new challenges and we can only hope to be prepared for the opportunities that those present if we are looking forward and upward rather than working with our heads down and grinding out some steady progress toward a goal that was out-of-date the day it was established. Fluid goals and objectives are messy and hard to measure and they are difficult to incorporate into institutional compensation and reward schemes, but the fact that they are challenging and complicated only means that the businesses and the institutions that first master these new approaches and systems and build upon them will be the ones that lead all of us forward.

So our businesses and our schools need to change and change quickly. But not without first understanding that there are major systemic barriers to effective change which need to be addressed and changed as well before real progress and improvement can occur. Otherwise, the very nature of the inquiries and the initiatives adopted will be uninformed by the right analysis and information and pedestrian at best. They will be just about as effective as the drunk looking for his keys under the street lamp – not because he thinks he lost them there – but because the light's better.

FENCE IT AND FORGET IT

It's the beginning of 2015 - a new budget year for many businesses - and - for a whole bunch of us - this means the start of another painful year of trying to live with a bunch of made-up numbers which – in all likelihood – aren't really even of our own making. They're driven by all kinds of external considerations including, but not limited to, the requirements of management; the needs and demands of investors; and, frankly, by the apparently universal belief that every new year's numbers need to be bigger and better than the prior year because – contrary to the scientific evidence – in the start-up fantasy world - apparently trees still can grow to the sky.

So you can look forward to twelve more months of trying to make someone else's dreams (or delusions) come true. Sorry to be bursting your bubble so soon in the season, but now's the time when it's still possible to have some honest conversations with the appropriate parties and to make some simple adjustments and changes in your projections and budgets that will make everyone's life a lot easier and more rational and – most likely – will also make for better ultimate results and happier folks as well.

Now I understand the need for ongoing growth (although some companies these days would do a lot better to slow down their growth efforts until they could convincingly demonstrate to someone that there was a profitable bottom line and eventually some brighter light at the end of the tunnel) and I also appreciate how the whole annual planning "process" works as well as anyone. So my problem isn't with the basic procedures; it's with some of their most central and sorely misguided underlying assumptions.

We go about the budgeting process in the same way each season and we never seem to learn – even with the demonstrable results staring us right in the face year after year – that: (a) not every aspect of any business can be defined, measured and documented in the same way (one financial or analytical approach – for sure – doesn't fit all) and (b) not everything in a business can be predicted or calculated in advance with mathematical precision because – try as we might to prevent it – sometimes the world and the people in it just have other plans. But we soldier on and everyone plays the same game of making forecasts (with an occasional wink on the side) and the numbers get generated and rolled out and that's when the real problems start. Because even though <u>we</u> all know that these are "best guesses" at best; too many people on the outside take them for gospel. They seem to have forgotten that saying alone doesn't make anything so.

Sure you had "input" and you told everyone that there were a lot of uncertainties again this year and the bean counters listened very attentively (and even sympathetically for a while) to your suggestions and advice, but ultimately when the rubber hit the road and - whether you liked it or not, they needed some concrete numbers from you to plug into their big old spreadsheets so they could crank out the upcoming year's budget documents, it turned out that they weren't leaving your office without them or willing to take "I don't know" for an answer. So you held your nose, bit your tongue, and did your best at making a few wild-ass final guesses to fill in those nasty gaps in the numbers. And then you went about the rest of your day hoping that the numbers wouldn't eventually come back to bite you. But you didn't feel good about it. And that's the rub. It's hard in your heart to sign up for a story which you yourself don't believe and it's even harder to execute. Even your most fervent prayers won't help because you can't pray a lie.

So, is there a better way? Can we fix even a small part of the problem and save ourselves a lot of pain in the process? I think so. I say – especially where we are dealing with matters that are demonstrably beyond anyone's ability to predict or control – that we just admit to that simple fact and adopt a new strategy which I call the "fence it and forget it" approach. It's clean, straightforward, ridiculously easy to administer and – as a bonus – it leads to results which are likely to be far closer to the eventual truth which makes it much easier for everyone to get a good night's sleep because they're not worrying about things they can't really do anything about.

And, while you will have to decide for yourself which are the best situations in which to apply it, I can guarantee that, once you get the hang of it, you'll never look back regardless of what kind of business you're in. Let me give you two radically different cases as examples from each end of the spectrum. The first is a church which runs a soup kitchen and tries every year to keep up with the growing and unpredictable demands of its clients and the second is a sales business where expensively wining and dining the buyers is still the way the game is played.

Case One – The Churches

Yep, even a church needs to have a budget and watch its expenses. But when it's crunch time and it's freezing cold outside; no one gets turned away or goes hungry at the soup kitchen - regardless of the budget or the best laid plans. That's just not the way the world works. And so, year after year, the end is always the same. It's sorta shame on the operators because it ended up costing more than they had planned to feed all the folks who showed up. Of course, everyone knows that no one knows how many folks you're gonna have to feed until the year's over. But nonetheless, the board blames you for spending too much to do too good a job of doing your job.

Case Two – The Clubs

No one ever said it was easy to manage your sales team's T & E expense line or to make sure that every meal really mattered and helped to make a sale. Or to determine (whatever the post-trip Salesforce notes may have said) that every trip needed to be taken to close a deal or to keep a customer close. And believe me, you can drive yourself and your team crazy sweating the small stuff like this. And that's really the point – it's small potatoes in the grand scheme of things and you can't let it get under your skin. Worrying about whether $50,000 over the course of a year is going to be pissed away on drinks and dinners when you're trying to make your company's first $15 million year in top line revenues a reality is a waste of your time which – well-spent - is worth a lot more than the measly $50k.

So what's the solution in both cases? You're worried about the sales guys taking too many trips? Take your best guess at what the number and costs should be – add 5% to be safe – and tell them that that's all they get for the year and it's on them to make it work. Same deal for the pantry – try your best to estimate the volumes and the costs – set the best budget amounts you can and add a small cushion and then you're done. That's the number and now it's mainly in God's hands.

What have you done? You put the problem in a box – you fenced it in – and then you were able to forget about it and focus on the much more important things that really matter. It's simply (1) constraining the problem and then (2) being content to live with the consequences and then, most importantly, (3) forgetting about it. We've got to all learn to live with some conscious and intentional ambiguity in our businesses if we want to make them better in the long run. We just can't sweat all the small stuff.

Now I know that this idea – conscious ambiguity and cost indifference – will make all my most anal and controlling friends (and every accountant in the city) anxious, but we've just got to admit it. We don't know everything and never will – we can't find out everything even after the fact – we can't predict everything (and wouldn't that be boring anyway?) – and we can't control everything. So what. Get over it and pay attention to the important stuff and to the places where you can make a real difference.

Here's What You Do.

(1) You pick some categories and you determine a budget number for each – your very best guess. You put the numbers out there for the team.

(2) You make it clear that these are serious numbers (but not written in stone) and that you expect everyone on the team to live with these numbers and try to make them real, but you don't kid yourself or them about it or obsess about it every day.

(3) You let the chips fall where they may throughout the year and you spend your days doing what really matters.

(4) Next year, you can take a look back and see whether the numbers need adjusting. It never hurts to be a better estimator as you learn.

(5) You congratulate yourself on how much less stressful your day seems now that you not concerned with policing all these petty matters or worried about a few bucks one way or the other – cause that's all these things will ever mean to your bottom line.

Here's Why You Do it.

(1) You do it to put an end – once and for all – to all the false precision and made-up metrics that used to creep into your budgets and destroy whatever real credibility and integrity they may have had. Once everyone knows that no one knows for sure – that it's always our best honest guesses, it's a lot easier for people to put their heads down and

go for the gold because everyone's in the same boat pulling in the same direction.

(2) You do it to give your team the clear message that you have confidence in them and that you trust them to make the right choices and decisions in the field and in the moment that no rule book and no budget will ever be able to address in advance. Because it's a real plan and a real budget, everyone can buy into it and take ownership and responsibility for the numbers – not lay them off as someone else's concern – and "owners" at any level in your business are exactly the folks you want minding the stores and pinching the pennies whenever they can.

(3) You do it because you've got much bigger fish to fry. No one likes to waste money – whoever's money it is – and so when you see that kind of behavior going on in your business – it's not about the money – it's a message to you and the rest of management that those folks don't feel good about the business and that's the real problem that you've got to fix. You won't see it or be able to recognize and fix it if you wandering thru the weeds worried about nickels and dimes.

IT'S REALLY HARD TO HIDE IN PLAIN SIGHT

I spoke recently about the impact of technology, connectivity and social media on the real estate business at a series of events sponsored by various brokerage companies and industry associations involved in the commercial (non-residential) real estate marketplace. These were very interesting forums because – while there's obviously a great deal of interest and concern among the key players and a real thirst for knowledge – I also came away with the feeling that the actual appetite for change was tempered in many instances by the idea that change was a good thing as long as the change was something that happened to somebody else.

A consistent inquiry in all of the Q & A sessions that followed my comments was how I expected the new technologies to alter the traditional and highly-personalized ways in which this type of business had been conducted for decades. You may think that the real estate business is all about "location, location, and location," but - in the final analysis - it's actually about continued confidence in the people you rely upon and longtime trusted relationships. And the one thing that we know for certain these days about trust and relationships is that the rise of social media and the constant presence of cell phones has been brutally difficult on both. It's really hard to hide in plain sight.

In my responses, I spoke about a variety of developing trends and oncoming changes including the need for a new type of employee – a digital native if you will - with the requisite attitudes and skill sets to be able to successfully function in an industry which was in the process of rapidly moving from a relationship-based world of intentional opacity to a bright, new and deeply democratized world of improved information, high degrees of visibility and data-driven decision-making.

I went on to say that this wasn't a thing about the age of the new players – it was about their willingness to adopt the emerging technologies and the newly-available tools and it didn't really matter whether the "newbies" were book smart or street smart as long as they understood how they would need to operate in the new digital world dictated by the twin agents of ubiquitous mobility and pervasive connectivity where every participant in any transaction had ready access to timely and relevant data.

But – in the overall flood of interesting and occasionally fearful questions – there was a single question – asked without the slightest hesitation or apparent discomfort – which really stood out from all of the rest. The truth is that what this long-time broker asked me was much more of an amazing admission by him rather than a question for me which is why I found it to be so interesting. I think it's also why so many others in the audience – brokers, builders, owners, lessors and lawyers – squirmed just a little bit and found the conversation to be somewhat uncomfortably close to home.

His question was short: My entire livelihood depends on the inefficiencies in the real estate market and ill-informed clients. How does my future look?

My first reaction was to think back to the early days of the computer business. We used to say that the primary difference between a used car salesman and a computer salesman was that at least the car dealer knew he was lying to you. Here was a broker saying that his success basically depended on the relative ignorance and lack of market knowledge of his clients.

Then I thought of that economist clown (and MIT professor) who was quoted as saying that the Affordable Care Act was purposely drafted by the Obama team with intentionally confusing language that was carefully designed to take advantage of "the stupidity of the American voter." Another arrogant academic moron who obviously feels far superior to the mere mortals who pay his salary. You really have to wonder how exactly these people live with themselves? But I digress.

In any case, I told the broker who asked that question that he was screwed. I didn't add: "as well you should be," but that wasn't really lost on anyone in the crowd. And please understand that this isn't especially about integrity in many cases. I think it's just a human condition in too many people who think that - as long as "good enough" is sufficient - they don't have to invest the time, energy and hard work that it takes to do the best possible job for their clients. They're willing to settle for doing just the kind of job that gets them through the day - especially because they believe that the clients don't know any better. But, from today on, the game's really changing because the clients will know a lot better and insist on a lot more. And that's what's so exciting (and so scary and threatening) to so many.

In the brave new world, asymmetrical information-based relationships will be a thing of the past and a fair assumption will be that everyone who cares will know anything that matters and that they should. Two words say it all: transparency and efficacy. The smart players today (buyers, sellers, clients and consumers) want to know as much as they can about every aspect of the conversations/transactions that impact them and they're going to increasingly insist on direct and immediate access to all of the relevant data. And then, when the data dust settles, they're going to make their choices, selections and decisions based on real metrics, real visibility and real bottom line results.

The players who prevail going forward won't be masters of the shell games, bait and switches, and other tricks of the trade that used to be the way things were done – they'll be the ones who are upfront, out front and leading the charge to the future where the best economic deals for the clients will prevail and where the chips will fall where they should – not because of ignorance and a lack of good information, but because of diligence, dedication and a lot of hard work.

IGNORANCE MASQUERADING AS OPINION

"There is nothing more frightful than ignorance in action."

(Goethe)

I was thinking about these poseurs who call themselves "opinion journalists" and what an oxymoron that is and, more importantly, how these halfwits must make the skins of the sadly shrinking population of real journalists crawl.

I realize that it's a source of very cheap labor (and these publishers are certainly getting what they're paying for), but I still have this old-fashioned view that even stupid and Iil-formed opinions ought to be based on some semblance of real inquiry and some modest factual basis rather than random rants written to order and based on factoids and fiction.

Sure I understand that it's quicker and easier just to make these "opinions" up (forget being there or doing any of the real research) and to claim to be relying on someone else's reporting - especially when you're trying to juggle a few too many commitments all at the same time.

And I also get that there's nothing easier in this media-crazed world than to find someone willing to say whatever you need said for whatever reasons and in support of whatever agenda they may have. But that's no better than just talking to yourself and certainly no more helpful or instructive. In fact, having these people just stand in front of a mirror and talk to themselves might be the least damaging and most narcissistically satisfying thing that they can do.

All of this wouldn't matter except that - as we continue to dilute and degrade what passes for journalism - it becomes harder and harder with a straight face to tell our kids that thoughtful, intelligent and civilized public discourse and the aggressive discussion of competing ideas and viewpoints is one of the most important foundations of our democracy.

We want our kids to learn to think and reason - not to rant - like the naysayers trying to sell newspapers (though thankfully not for much longer) or the bozos on cable or in Congress. Children and young adults today are facing an unprecedented flood of indiscriminate information (and a bunch of crappy, one-sided opinions as well) and they need to learn how to filter the flow, evaluate the relative strengths and weaknesses of the various positions, and ultimately decide what they believe.

This isn't rocket science, but it is a scientific process and it's one that is just beginning to be taught in some of our schools and it's gonna rock the very foundations of our educational system because it's about teaching our kids how to think and think for themselves rather than memorizing a bunch of conventional wisdom spewed by a "sage on the stage" which may or may not have any real value for them in the future.

As I have watched some of our EDtech companies at 1871 (especially *ThinkCERCA*) roll these new programs out to schools, it has been a joy and a wonder to see how quickly the students adopt the new approach and move from passively sitting back as the old wisdom washes over and right past them to leaning into this new world where they actively take control and responsibility for constructing arguments and building the foundations for their own education. Tell me - I might listen. Show me - I might learn. But let me do it myself and I own it for life.

Watching the kids using *ThinkCERCA*'s tools to build their arguments step by step starting with their <u>Claim</u> – then gathering the <u>Evidence</u> for it – then explaining their <u>Reasoning</u> for it – next addressing the <u>Counter Arguments</u> – and doing it all in <u>Language</u> appropriate to their audiences is an amazing experience. You can just feel the difference – they're taking responsibility and control and ownership – and it shows in their posture, in their faces, and in the results. This is exciting stuff and the sad sacks that call themselves journalists could learn a lot from these kids who actually know whereof they speak.

YOU DON'T KNOW SHINOLA

Tom Kartsotis and his brother Kosta built *Fossil* (FOSL) from scratch starting in 1984 (when Tom dropped out of college and was scalping football tickets in Texas) and turning into a global lifestyle brand and a public company with 14,000 employees which - 30 years later - sells $3.2 billion worth of bags, watches and clothing a year and has a market cap of more than $5 billion.

Tom retired as the Chairman of *Fossil* in 2010 and these days Kosta runs the *Fossil Group* while Tom (through his private equity firm – Bedrock Manufacturing) has turned his primary attention to a new challenge – *Shinola* (www.shinola.com) - an analog watch manufacturing and marketing start-up in a profoundly digital world. With 7 retail stores, close to 400 employees making great wages, and an exploding online demand as well for its products which now include multiple lines of watches, high-end bicycles and other accessories, the company is well-positioned to help Detroit and to create the next big lifestyle brand. And, amazingly enough, it's really just getting started.

The Kartsotis brothers are pretty private guys and rarely – if ever – talk to the press or any other media. They understand the power and importance of getting their brand and their "story" out there, but they prefer to do it guerilla-style and face-to-face rather than through the traditional channels. So Tom and some other key members of his team (including **Shinola** President Jacques Panis) agreed recently to sit down with me and a couple of dozen of our 1871 entrepreneurs in our Chicago startup incubator to give us the inside scoop on **Shinola.**

Tom shared some of the lessons they've already learned (as the company nears its third year of existence) in building a "new" manufacturing business in an era of high-tech and digital everything; he talked about the size of the opportunities they see ahead of them and the openings and market gaps that they are targeting; and he answered a bunch of questions from the founders of some of our own most exciting startups. There were plenty of concrete take-aways that were relevant to every entrepreneur in the room and I've summarized a few of the most important ones below.

I Wish I Could Say That We Had A Plan.

Sometimes you just have to believe, get the process started and have confidence that - with a lot of effort and persistence - you will get there – even when you're not exactly sure where there is. It helps a lot to have a vision and a dream and a compelling story. Shinola is about pride and craft, making things that matter and last, and honoring our past as well as the future. It's a no nonsense notion combined with a lot of nostalgia and it's the real deal. No one believed the **Shinola** team when they explained what they intended to do (to start a watch factory in a 100-year old office building in Detroit) and Tom thinks that there are still some folks out there shaking their heads, but now they're wearing **Shinola** watches and riding their **Runwell** bikes. He also noted that there will surely be bumps in the road and false starts which you'll simply have to manage through. He said that they've had plenty of hiccups, but they just kept their heads down and plowed ahead. Nobody ever said building a new business was easy. He pointed out that their idea for a Tall Men's store in Tokyo didn't work out real well – but he was just kidding.

If We Take Care Of Our People, They'll Take Care Of Our Customers And Our Business.

Shinola pays its people well; provides amazing medical benefits; and even pays them above-market wages while training them right in their own factory. Everyone spends time in the company's retail stores because listening to the customers is the best feedback you'll ever get. But – far more importantly – *Shinola* believes and shows everyone that anyone can succeed if they're willing to work hard and put in the time and effort that is required. The company celebrates their successes and some of the most important team members – who started with *Shinola* as guards, janitors, delivery people, etc. – are now in charge of critical parts of the operations and continuing to grow and learn more every day. Success breeds success and believing that your people are your most important asset and that they can always be better is the only way to keep raising the bar.

We Start With The Best Product We Can Find (Or Imagine) And Then Make The Numbers Work.

If you aim for the stars and being the best you can be, you very often get there. If you ask people why not and why something can't be done a new way; you'd be surprised how often you get the answers and the results you looking for. The Shinola team brought in the best Swiss watch builders in the world to train their people. They built a first-class factory that's as clean as a surgery suite. And they guaranteed their products for life. These aren't small hurdles or tentative commitments – these guys are all-in, but they also understand that they've got to make the numbers work for the long term so that the businesses can scale. It's reverse engineering on steroids and a fierce attention to every production detail and source of materials and it's opening up new opportunities for the company and its many U.S.-based supply partners. **Shinola** believes that - penny for penny and pound for pound, their people can learn to build better products at competitive costs with far higher quality in Detroit than are now being manufactured anywhere else in the world.

If Your High Prices Are Propped Up By Huge Marketing Spends, You're Ripe For Disruption.

The traditional high-end luxury watch industry has benefitted from enormous mark-ups and margins which are largely dependent on the manufacturers' very substantial brand advertising and marketing spends. **Shinola** saw an open space in the market and an opportunity to offer a high quality product at price points which were still very profitable and yet only a fraction of the pricing which the traditional brands were maintaining through their massive ad campaigns. The **Shinola** team believed that you can make a great product and a great living (and even give back to your community) without being greedy and taking advantage of the consumer. These days the **Shinola** watches are the entry point into the higher-end, luxury watch sector of the business even while they are also seen by consumers as solid, workman-like, precision products suitable for everyone.

It's not easy to be all things to all people, but it appears that everyone knows and loves **Shinola**.

ARE ENTREPRENEURS BORN OR BUILT OR BOTH?

I was part of a recent Oxford-style debate in Chicago where the proposition under consideration was that "Entrepreneurs are born, not trained." It was the classic nature versus nurture type of heated argument between two pairs of seasoned senior executives and serial entrepreneurs. And truth be told, I think that each of the advocates in the debate (except maybe my debate partner, Amy Wilkinson) could have easily argued in favor of or against either side of the proposition. Amy herself was pretty hardcore on our side of the argument (we were the "built" team) and she had some pretty strong ammunition as well based on her most recent research in the field.

In fact, the entire contest was especially informed and influenced by Amy's participation since she (after 5 years of serious investigation interviewing dozens of hugely-successful company founders) had just published a new book on entrepreneurs called *The Creator's* Code. I'd say it's a must read for anyone who wants to understand what it takes to survive and succeed in the startup world. I don't want to try to summarize it because I couldn't do it justice and because the many concrete examples in the book which are drawn from one-on-one conversations with all of these people are invaluable additions to the book's own concrete conclusions. But – as noted below –

while you definitely need the big names and boffo stories to move the books off the shelves, the real value of her years of diligent research and analysis is how the findings can help all of us everyday entrepreneurs be better at accomplishing what we're trying to do.

Amy's book identifies and describes a cluster of distinct abilities that will sound very familiar to any serious entrepreneur, but it also makes the more interesting assertion that real break-through success depends on the presence, not of some of these talents and capabilities, but of ALL of them at the same time and in the same person. Her research shows that every one of the six essential skills which she had identified were present in each and every one of the male and female entrepreneurs in her study.

The underlying study basically focused on the founders of companies which had reached $100 million or more in revenues over a 5 year period. Rapidly growing and highly impactful companies. Every one of the founders she spent time with is a household name today to millions of people, but not a single one of them would call themselves an overnight success. Nor would they say (even though the premise of the book is their skill sets) that they achieved their successes alone. And, in fact, one of the six essential skills is the ability to network and draw talent and resources to your ideas. These narratives are all about striving, persistence, passion and even patience which is something we rarely talk about in this context, but it's invaluable to understand that you should never confuse a clear view of where you're headed with the time or distance that it will take to get there or how difficult the journey will be.

Amy's research also demonstrated that the more times a given individual exercised these abilities and the more businesses he or she created over time, the better they got each time at the process and the higher the likelihood that they would again be massively successful. Practice and application make increasingly perfect. Perhaps the prime poster boy (and serial entrepreneur) in the book is Elon Musk for obvious reasons – although, as she noted – nothing was sure or obvious (except his raw intelligence) when he started and – in fact – Elon faced the abyss multiple times in several of his most successful ventures, but he never stopped believing. By his own admission, he taught himself a great deal about a number of different industries and, throughout his journey, he learned immense amounts from each and every bump in the road. The bottom line of Amy's research and the most compelling conclusion was that all of these critical tools and techniques can be <u>learned</u>, honed, and improved upon throughout anyone's career and over successive instances of starting new businesses.

Note that I use the term "learned" rather than "taught" because so many of the individuals in Amy's study were not classically advantaged or trained in the areas of their ultimate triumphs. In fact, they were almost all more scrappy and "street smart" than brilliant or "book smart" in the areas that really mattered to their eventual businesses. This distinction – of course – became a major bone of contention in the debate itself. Our view was that becoming an effective entrepreneur and a business success was about experience, iteration, and learned craft (as well as a full measure of good fortune) rather than some genetically-determined destiny that inescapably assured you of eventual success. At the outset of the debate, the audience was informally polled and they agreed substantially (60-40) with our side of the argument. The trick was not to lose them over the course of the discussion.

Our opponents immediately attempted to pigeonhole us in the academic world and repeatedly stressed that their view of the "training" under discussion was the type that could only take place in the narrowest confines of colleges, universities and graduate programs. We countered that they were attempting to make a distinction which made no real difference in the real world. Where and how you gained and developed the skills didn't matter a bit – the point was that none of these talents appears fully-realized and ready to roll at birth or at the outset of anyone's careers.

As you might expect, there was a lot of loose talk about crazy people, college dropouts, about people happy to take insane risks, about fatal optimists, and about the absolute cream of the crop – those few super entrepreneurs whose names we all know and revere. But, when the dust settled, the thing that struck me at the end of the contest was that we are actually doing so many aspiring entrepreneurs a real disservice by focusing on the very few Michael Jordans and the Lang Langs of business (who may be amazing or may just be the luckiest people alive at the right time and right place) rather than on the thousands of equally successful (if considerably smaller) entrepreneurs who are working just as hard everyday to build their businesses and who can really learn and demonstrably benefit the most from the important lessons which Amy's book has to share.

Uber is a great story, but the real growth and expansion of new businesses and the creation of new jobs will come from the hundreds of businesses that apply the new lessons of the sharing economy and "*Uberize*" their own businesses and industries. Similarly, there will be *Airbnb*-ish solutions brought forward in many market sectors. All of these successes will be driven by individuals who master and intelligently apply all of the essential skills which Amy sets out in her book to their own enterprises and not by the ones who think that the key to success is to emulate Travis or Zuck by rocking a hoodie and then sitting by the roadside waiting for the lightning to strike. Hope is not a strategy for success. Hard work, perseverance and iteration are.

Finally, in the interests of full disclosure, I have to confess that by the discussion's end – due in no small part – to the under-handed and reprehensible behavior of our opponents (and some pithy comments about the height of NBA players and other flagrant grandstanding), the audience was somewhat swayed in favor of our opponent's position and the gap in opinion was narrowed although we ultimately prevailed in a purely mathematical sense. Small solace.

WHAT OUR KIDS SHOULD LEARN IN SCHOOL

It turns out – in a perfect world – that much of what every kid would ideally learn in school is, in part, a working familiarity with the same attitudes, approaches and outlooks which we try to have our aspiring 1871 entrepreneurs internalize as a lasting part of their overall experience with us.

Today, there's no question that we learn a great deal through indirect lateral learning which comes principally from our observations of the trials and tribulations (and the successes and failures) of the others around us who are engaged in similar or parallel activities. Not only does misery love company; the fact is that the cheapest and least painful education available today is making sure that you don't repeat someone else's mistakes while you're building your business. In addition, peer-to-peer communications are a constant and growing part of our lives and thus we also learn every day directly from each other and from others across the globe.

When you combine these new knowledge sources with the many independent media and content channels which are now readily and continually available to all of us, it's increasingly clear that most of us are learning as much or more from the digital universe as we have to date or will hereafter learn from any traditional and/or formal education programs.

And, although the debate continues to rage as to which startup skills can be <u>taught</u>, it's very clear that a great deal can be <u>learned</u> by new business builders who immerse themselves in the critical and creative entrepreneurial mass which an incubator like 1871 provides – especially when all of the other component parts of the startup ecosystem are also present in the same physical location – including hundreds of other new entrepreneurs, universities, VCs, experienced serial entrepreneurs and committed mentors, angel investors, city and state representatives, substantial educational resources and programming, alumni businesses, etc.

But we need to figure out exactly how to make sure that the policies and programs in our schools are designed and organized in ways which help our kids learn these same entrepreneurial life skills as early and as fully as possible. It's not about filling their heads with ancient philosophies and rote facts; it's about filling their hearts with a passion for learning and the desire to make a difference – to make their efforts and their lives meaningful - both in the near term and in the long run. And it's a process which can't be started too soon.

Here are the top 10 "need to knows" on my list and a brief comment on each:

(1) <u>You Get What You Work for, Not What You Wish for</u>

In the real world, effort trumps talent and inspiration without execution means nothing. Our attitude is that, while we may not always outsmart the other guys, we will always out-prepare and outwork them.

(2) Keep Raising the Bar

Successive approximation beats postponed perfection. The fact is that you get better by getting better and you do that by constantly raising the bar and iterating like mad. In a world of fast followers and global competition, we want to always be on the move and moving forward.

(3) Shoot for the Stars

If you don't ask, you never get. Someone is gonna be first and grab the best seat in the place and it might as well be you, but not if you don't go for it. As Michael Jordan used to say: you miss 100% of the shots you don't take. And, if you don't bother to ask, the answer's always "No".

(4) Don't Sell Yourself Short

There are always plenty of people who will tell you why you can't do something – mainly because they haven't tried or couldn't do it themselves. Don't allow yourself to be defined or constrained by other people's limitations. Ya never know whether you can do it until you try. And every day the people who are doing it are blowing by the ones who insist that it can't be done.

(5) Start Now with What You Have

Waiting for the perfect moment and all the stars to align won't get you anywhere and waiting for a schedule or permission will get you left in the dust by the people who are just getting out there and getting things done. Nothing will ever get done if every objection and problem needs to be resolved before you start. The time will never be just right, but the time to start is always "now".

(6) Nobody said Life was Fair

Sometimes things just don't work out. The best entrepreneurs understand that no one makes all the right choices or decisions – the trick is to learn from all of them – good or bad – and to not make the same mistakes over again. And, while hard work is necessary for success, it's not sufficient in itself or any certain guarantee. Luck, timing, tools, the quality and commitment of your team, etc. – all of these are also success factors. And even when everything aligns, there are still too many instances to count where the world seems to have conspired to kill your dream. This is why resilience and the ability to get over the past and get on with the future are just as crucial as the perseverance that it often takes to stick with your idea through thick and thin. Fall down three times; get up four times.

(7) Never Play the Blame Game

People can always find an excuse or blame their circumstances for why things didn't happen or work out the way they hoped. But the ones who will always succeed are the ones who take whatever they are handed and make those conditions and constraints work. Hoping for something better isn't an effective strategy – it's just a formula for further disappointment. When you start blaming others for your problems, you give up your power and the ability to make critical changes.

(8) It's Only a "No" for Now

Winners keep pressing and never take "No" for a final answer – just an opportunity to try harder. Excellence and real results are always based ultimately in perseverance – sticking around long enough so that even if you can't win them over, at least you will eventually wear down their resistance. There are no shortcuts or tricks to make the path easier and there's no finish line either.

(9) Sometimes the Baby Just is Ugly

Kids who think they'll live forever (and who are frankly too young to even understand the consequences of many of their actions) have no concept of opportunity costs or the fact that your time is probably the scarcest resource you have. Sadly, it's often the same kind of problem with passionate, but inexperienced young entrepreneurs. They stick with things way too long and end up beating a dead horse when they should be moving on. They regularly forget the first rule of holes: when you're in one, stop digging.

(10) Make Something that Makes a Difference

It's hard to get out of your own head when you're young, but it's never too early to explain the value of being connected to something – a cause, an idea, a team, etc. – that's bigger than yourself. At 1871, we say that you can't be in this stuff for the money – it's just too hard and it's really not about making money or even about making a living. It's about making a life worth living and one that makes a difference and a contribution to others.

SILICON WADI DOCUMENTARY

Straight from the heart of the Startup Nation, this very frank and realistic film is an important cautionary tale for everyone who imagines that they want to start a business or be an entrepreneur.

The clear and consistent message is that it's very hard to do this kind of work and that it's not just hard on the entrepreneurs, but it's equally as difficult (or more so) on their families as well. Before any wanna-be starts down this path, you need to ask yourself (as well as the people you care the most about) the very same question that you should ask before you loan money to a close friend – which is the most important – and which are you prepared to lose? I tell all our entrepreneurs that there's always more work, but you've only got one family. Building a new business is a 24/7 job and there's no way to leave anything at the office at the end of the day because the day never ends.

The second important message from the film is that it's pretty easy to convince yourself of just about anything – convincing investors and customers that you have something real and different and important is a much more challenging job. There are only a few people who will care enough to tell you the truth and that's especially true when the truth hurts. But the truth only hurts (as you'll see throughout the film) when it ought to. It's never easy to say what no one wants to hear.

You'll also hear a recurring refrain from Yosi as he explains how his idea for Fiddme came to him. This really bothered me. He keeps saying that he thought to himself in that moment: "I think we have a startup." But no one who knows anything wants to hear that. Saying "I think we have a business is good." Saying "I think we've found a pain point and a solution" is better. And saying "I think we have lots of people willing to pay for our product or service" is best of all. We've got tons of startups today – what we're looking for are sustainable businesses. Cash is important, but customers are king.

And, if you listen closely, you'll hear the venture capitalist David Blumberg explain a very critical concept in the startup world. Being a little early is OK, but being too early means you die. And here's a little known fact – the largest single determinant of startup success is timing – not the idea, not the team, and not the funding. You've got to be in the right place at the right time for lightning to strike. And it also helps a whole bunch to be lucky.

I wasn't crazy about how one of the stories ended (no spoiler alert is required here) because it confirmed one of the worst possible messages in our business which is that it's better to be lucky than smart or hard-working. In fact, there's a great new book out by Randall Lane called: "You Only Have to be Right Once" which tells the stories of our latest crop of a dozen tech billionaires and leaves you with the exact same impression – that with the possible exception of Mark Zuckerberg – the rest of the new breed of superhero entrepreneurs could just as easily have been driving a cab these days or working as a computer technician.

And the final, very instructive, message (mainly for Israelis rather than U.S.-based entrepreneurs) is that it's a stupid waste of time and effort to go from Tel Aviv to the Valley looking for your pot of gold. Cash is everywhere in the states these days, but much more than capital, businesses need customers to succeed and there are NO customers on the Coast. If you want to build a real business, you need to be where the buyers are and that's in places like Chicago and not San Francisco.

One last thought which I think the film also makes clear – it's a hard life and a bumpy road for sure – but for a certain breed of person – it's the only way to live. We spend a great deal of our lives working and the greatest privilege and joy there is .. is to be able to get up every day and do something that you can be excited and enthusiastic about.

IF YOU CAN DO IT, IT AIN'T BRAGGIN'

I've been saying for a while now that there's a problem with the classic definition of insanity which basically maintains that - if you insist on only doing things the ways you have always done them, it's crazy to expect better or different results. Otherwise stated, it's simply an acknowledgment that "to get what we've never had, we're going to have to do what we've never done." We hear a lot of this talk, but – especially in larger businesses – it's mainly just that – a lot of talk and wishful thinking and not much else. And part of the reason may be that the traditional formulation itself has worn out its welcome. It's not enough to simply be a new or different way of doing the same old things; the new solutions need to be bigger, broader and better all-around in order to make a real difference.

One simple solution for the perception part of the problem may be for these traditional businesses to look at the way the smartest startups view the world. To the guys still sitting quietly in the C suites with their fingers and toes crossed who are hoping that this web/digital thing will just blow over like some many other fads before it blows up in their faces or seriously beats up their bottom lines – especially during their time in the hot seat - I would simply say: if you really want things to stay the way they are, they're gonna have to change. And change dramatically and change soon.

Simply looking at past actions, present plans, capabilities and resources, and/or the actions of direct and obvious competitors isn't a sufficient inquiry any longer. Incremental improvements may change the results by a few cents or goose this quarter's market share by a point or two, but they're not going to alter the game anymore. Looking for tweaks and short-term improvements is just too narrow a perspective and far too limited an approach to succeed in the new world of global competitors – many of whom aren't saddled with your legacy systems or the need to support the old enterprise offerings while the customers want tomorrow's technologies.

In today's disruptive and discontinuous world, this constricted view isn't especially helpful or instructive because it has us all looking backwards or laterally instead of looking ahead. Our job today is to desire, expect and demand more than what others - and the world at large - thinks is possible. At 1871, we like to say that, if you don't know it's impossible, it's that much easier to do. And, of course, things always seem impossible to the naysayers until they get done and then they belatedly seem obvious.

So, if we limit ourselves to what has come before or benchmark ourselves solely against the known competition, we are bounding our opportunities by the limitations of those around us. That's simply too low a bar. Just because they can't or haven't done something doesn't remotely suggest that we should take on those boundaries or that we can't do much more. The ways things have always been done aren't the upper limits of what's possible or achievable - they're just what's come before - supported and calcified by the tired and conventional wisdom.

There are countless ways that we fall into this mindless way of thinking, but one that seems to be uncommonly common is the way we have historically regarded and identified our competition and, more importantly, how we organize ourselves to address and deal with them.

Values, Ethics & Failure in the Digital Age

Large businesses have traditionally regarded their primary markets as zero-sum environments with the attitude that it was their job to take as much market share away from their competitors as possible. Basically, a "what's mine is mine and what's yours we can talk about" attitude. AT&T executives used to joke that they weren't a monopoly, they just enjoyed 100% customer loyalty. All these executives saw their world as a see-saw or a teeter-totter with compensating adjustments being made over time among the players. It was a "nice" world – things were predictable – things were consistent – things were reliable – and often it was a world governed by overt or indirect understandings and agreements as to price controls or price level maintenance arrangements which served the players' interests in maintaining high prices and avoiding price wars, but rarely, if ever, benefitted the customers or end users.

Today, almost every aspect of that world has changed. The customer is in the driver's seat and if you're not meeting his or her needs, they'll be gone in a flash. And those needs continue to regularly expand with a constantly rising bar. Good enough no longer is – the way you stay in the game is getting better all the time. And the competition looks a lot more like dodge-em cars than the see-saw because: (a) they're coming at you from every direction, not in a linear or direct fashion – and (b) their numbers, approaches, offerings and multi-channel delivery systems are exploding. It's not a fixed set of folks – it's not a gentlemen's game anymore – it's every business for itself and everyone wanting your business as well.

I've described this new world of opportunities – especially for new and nimble businesses – as one where there are so many new and different areas for aggressive and innovative companies to conquer that the real challenge is more about focus than anything else. You can extend your business into new areas – you can "slide to the side" into adjacent markets – you can offer alternatives to existing solutions – cheaper, faster, more accessible, etc. and you can create entirely new markets and products and services based on the new tools, mobility and connectivity which we now have.

None of this is remotely good news for the big guys, incumbents and the powers that be. In the absence of immediate action and changes in their own businesses, the best they can hope for is a slow and painful slide into oblivion. Or they can recognize that maintenance (or trying to just hold on) isn't a vision or a strategy for today. Today, you can't sit back and let things happen to you – you get better by getting started and getting better every day thereafter. It's fairly easy to understand, but ridiculously hard to consistently execute.

At 1871, we try to do it every day and we keep 3 objectives constantly in mind:

(1) Set Impossible Standards;

(2) Expend Extraordinary Efforts; and

(3) Achieve Remarkable Results.

Expect nothing less from yourself and your team and you'll be surprised at how well things will work out.

WHY ENTREPRENEURS ARE REALLY TERRIBLE AT SAYING THANK YOU

Who would have thought that there would be some worthwhile words of wisdom coming from Glinda, the Good Witch, in Wicked? I saw Wicked again recently for the umpteenth time and I was struck by how relevant some of the lyrics from the song were to the entrepreneurial mindset and to the ways many entrepreneurs behave. These pithy but poignant phrases were words that any struggling entrepreneur would recognize. And they are so timely as well, given that Thanksgiving is when we're all supposed to be so aggressively appreciative.

One of the things that we entrepreneurs don't do well is to say "thank you" fast enough or often enough to so many of the people that matter in our lives and who make our achievements possible. Not just thanks to our peers and team members, but to our friends, family, investors, advisors and mentors as well. Why is that? And why can't we do better? Sure, this could be a function of busy schedules and the fact that we're all in a hurry these days - although it's not actually that hard to be thankful and to take a minute or two to let someone know that you are. So that seems like a somewhat inadequate explanation. Praise and recognition are quick, easy and cost-effective ways to acknowledge and reward your team's contributions. And worth making time for. Success is definitely sweeter when it is shared.

But there are some deeper-seated startup psychologies at work and, while these aren't offered as excuses, at least they're a plausible explanation for some behaviors that don't otherwise make much personal or business sense. Frankly, entrepreneurs just aren't that conscientious about taking the time to say "thanks" to the people who helped them along the way. But I honestly don't think that this behavior is because most of us are unappreciative or simply ingrates.

I think it's more that we're uncomfortable and don't quite know how to handle these circumstances when we're thrust into the spotlight. Celebrations are so yesterday. They make you feel like your goals are behind you and that's just not how entrepreneurs look at the world. So we tend to clam up and try to soldier through the ceremonies, but our heads aren't really in the game. We're somewhat awkward, completely stuck in our own minds, and maybe a little tongue-tied in these cases because - in some respects - we just don't believe or buy into the whole process. And we're a little surprised to find ourselves in such a spot. It's a little hard to be gracious when your principal goal is to get off the stage.

In Wicked, Glinda is supposed to be joyously celebrating her engagement, but, as things progress and she sings about how "happy" she is, we hear more and more of a tone that suggests that she's got some very mixed feelings about what's going on around her. According to the crowd and the conventional wisdom, her "dreams" have all come true, but she's not so sure. She says that "it is, I admit, the tiniest bit unlike I anticipated".

And, instead of being a happy and simple time, "getting your dreams - it's strange, but it seems a little - well - complicated." She knows that she should be overjoyed and grateful, but she's not quite there yet. We've all been in similar circumstances - waiting for someone to pinch us to make sure things are real. And it's also a bit of the "dog that caught the car" syndrome. You finally grabbed the brass ring that you've been chasing for a while. Now what? And maybe even more importantly, you find yourself - just like Glinda - wondering what you had to give up in the process to get there.

Most of the best entrepreneurs I know would tell you that they do a lot better in tough times and in dealing with adversity than they do with success and when things are working out well. Success is a little like wine. It's just hard for a true entrepreneur to believe in it. You don't believe in wine. You drink it, enjoy it for a moment, and then you try to get on with your life. Entrepreneurs are superstitious and they want to get back to work before anyone notices and before anyone can snatch the moment away. For a lot of us who are confirmed paranoids, these "celebrations" are rarely joyous occasions. At best, they're waystations on what we expect to be a much longer and harder road ahead.

It also has something to do with authenticity as every returning vet will tell you. Only the guys actually in the trenches - the entrepreneurs themselves - really know how close to the line things got - how near to the edge they came - and how much luck (and even a little fear) had to do with the outcome. And only the entrepreneur knows all the sacrifices that it took to get there and how quickly these things can turn around and race in the wrong direction. Glinda says: "There's a kind of a sort of a cost. There's a couple of things get lost. There are bridges you cross you didn't know you crossed until you've crossed." These things are hard to share with folks who haven't been there.

And then there's this crazy idea that has you asking yourself exactly how big a deal it could be if you (of all people) are able to pull it off. It's a little hard to congratulate and thank your teammates when you're not sure whether you even deserve the credit in the first place. The battle's always far from over, there's no finish line - just another hill, and it's a lot more like sitting on tacks than it is resting on your laurels.

The world thinks that most entrepreneurs are beyond confident, if not arrogant, but the truth is that they're mostly scared little guys running full speed ahead, jumping over the potholes, and trying to look over both their shoulders to see who's coming up behind them to take their toys away.

Is it any wonder that they forget from time to time to say thank you for the honor?

STARTUP LESSONS FROM SUPER BOWL 50

For me the Super Bowl had so many of the unfortunate characteristics and reminders of the kinds of struggles that every startup goes thru that - by the game's anti-climactic end - it felt surprisingly like just another day at the office. It was more like an obligation than an opportunity. You had to watch it, but no one really expected that you would enjoy it. And the commercials were not much better. The game was much more of a sideways shuffle than a spectacular show and there certainly wasn't a lot of "joy in Mudville" for anyone on either team. It wasn't a thrilling competition between two super-closely matched competitors – it was more like a contest to see who could make the fewest mistakes and still put some points on the board. There's no passion in playing to avoid the potholes rather than shooting for the stars.

Building a business can feel like a similar grind for days and months on end, but those are the times that it pays to keep your head down and keep plowing straight ahead since that's what will make all the difference in the long run. Playing it safe – trying to straddle the middle – going for maintenance rather than majesty – all leads you to the same sorry state. This startup stuff is hard – it's not for the faint-hearted - and not everyone gets a trophy for trying really hard or a salute for showing up. You've got to set the bar high – model the necessary behavior every day – and never let them see you sweat. Anyone who tells you that being an entrepreneur is a lot of "fun" hasn't been there and is most likely lying to you. It can be thrilling and super satisfying; it can be exhilarating and enervating; it can also be downright lonely and depressing, but it's always work – not fun. Fun is what you theoretically do on your own time – as if there was such a thing in the startup world.

On Sunday the good news was that everyone survived - not too many injuries or concussions – but also not many points on the score board for long stretches - not a lot of glory plays or great stands or saves - and not exactly an inspiring contest likely to stir men's blood. It felt like the winners were more relieved to escape with their modest victory and some dignity than ecstatic about how they triumphed. And sometimes in the startup world, you can get to the end of a week where you wonder how you even made it through and ended up still standing only to discover that you didn't really accomplish a damn thing in terms of moving the business forward. The truth is that today it takes more than baby steps and incremental improvements to change the game and move the needle. The future isn't going to be incremental – it's going to be explosive. What we don't know is just whose efforts are going to be the ones that make the real differences – the hustlers, the hipsters or the hackers. But whatever the team consists of, it's headed nowhere without a leader that the rest of the folks can believe in.

I think in a way that some of the disappointed feeling that surrounded the conclusion of this grossly over-hyped "big game" is an unfortunate commentary on how hard it is in our stupid celebrity-soaked system to root for a great defense rather than celebrating an amazing offense. Just like in a startup, the sales guys get all the kudos for bringing home the bacon while the coders just catch a lot of crap when the system shuts down. No one said that life was fair, and the linemen always come last, but who honestly really remembers that the most important touchdown in Sunday's game was scored early on by the defense. If you're in it for the credit, you're in the wrong place. To win, on game day and in business, everyone has to show up and do the very best job that they can – regardless of their responsibility or position – and know that they helped make a difference. No one does anything major these days all by themselves.

I guess it just goes to show you that you and your own team had better learn to appreciate and take your everyday satisfaction from all the preparation, perspiration, passion and hard work that you put into what you're building together (which you desperately hope will be special) regardless of the near-term outcomes and results because the world in general doesn't really care and no one gives you any points in the end for trying. "Almost" counts in love and horseshoes, but not so much in the real world of business.

Worse yet, just as we saw in the game on too many occasions, what you've put together and pushed painfully forward in your business can also be pissed away in a matter of seconds. There were mistakes and mishaps galore, foolish errors and omissions, sacks and stupid choices, taunts and other bad behavior that killed critical drives, and wastes of hard-to-come-by momentum throughout the game - virtually everything we also see in the startup world every day.

Now I can pretty much forgive a fumble or a missed field goal because those almost never arise from a lack of trying. As often as not, the main cause of a fumble is because the runner was trying to press for a few more yards and gets stripped or hit so hard that he loses the ball. But a lack of commitment or a failure of leadership is something that no team or business can accept for long. It's corrosive and contagious. For me, the saddest thing about Sunday's Super Bowl wasn't Cam Newton dropping the ball; it was that he stood there (while America and the world watched with bated breath) and didn't throw himself into the fray. He was deciding, not diving. Looking, not lunging.

And we were all sitting at home on the edges of our seats screaming "go for it", "get the ball" and he didn't do a thing. In fact, I'd say that the key to the ultimate moral victory in the game (forget what the score ended up being) really came down to that single play - a few painful and probative seconds - which may not have changed the final outcome, but that forever changed my impression of Cam Newton. And I'm willing to bet it changed the impressions of millions of other viewers as well.

When the moment arose and he was tested, he didn't step up – he hesitated – or worse, he took a pass. Maybe it was heart that he didn't have. Maybe he was saving himself for next season. Maybe he just didn't want it as bad as we wanted him to. But, whatever the reasons or the excuses, it wasn't what we expect from our leaders, and it was a sobering lesson for any startup.

You can't lead from the back seat or the bleachers. You've got to be in the moment – all-in – showing your people and your team that you care more than other people think is smart or safe. That you demand of yourself and them more than others think is practical or possible. And that when the window is there and the opportunities arise; you'll be the first one through to take the chances and seize the moment.

PART II

FAILURE

WHAT NOBODY TELLS YOU ABOUT FAILURE

There are no skid marks when a start-up shuts down. If you think that it's hard to get a new business off the ground, you should really try shutting down a start-up or two in order to appreciate what serious stress means. If there's a lonelier and more depressing spot for a young entrepreneur to be in, I can't really imagine what it would be. Especially because there's rarely anyone – inside or outside of the business – and even at home - that you can talk to honestly about the prospect of closing your company down. Even your banker and your attorney will start to turn a little green around the gills and get that slightly vacant look in their eyes when the prospect is raised that they might not get paid or repaid. You'll find that their advice and answers slow down somewhat (it's like English is their second language and they have to translate stuff in their heads first before they speak it to you) and – all of a sudden - everything feels somewhat tentative. I realize that this kind of situation always sucks, but it's a fact of life and in the next year or two - as more and more start-ups run out of gas and out of runway because they can't raise their next round of financing – it's going to become a front-and-center concern for everyone who's active in any capacity in the early-stage investment space.

So get ready and, when it happens to you – directly or indirectly – wherever you happen to be in the food chain, don't start thinking that people are against you (or generally out to get you - although you could be pardoned for occasionally thinking that when things look especially dark), just try to remember that it's simply the fact that they're much more interested in looking out for themselves and their interests first and foremost than they are in going out on a limb to save your bacon. As they like to say, it's not personal; it's just business. But, of course, it's your life and your business that's on the line.

And it's you – and often you alone – who has to sit up at night and worry about when to pull the plug. By the way, after setting out to change the world and seeing that it's not happening, it takes just as much strength and courage to plug the plug as it did to set out on the journey in the first place. It's pretty easy to sign up new employees and talent when the till is full; it's a lot more challenging when you're inviting people to come on board what may be your version of the *Titanic*. And it's pretty easy to pump up the troops and send them out on critical sales calls when you know you've got the cash to cover their credit card charges. Not so much when they might be unknowingly bankrolling the business and when you know that that's the last thing they can afford to do if they'll be out of a job entirely in a couple of months. Things can get pretty darn ugly fast when you hit that slippery slope. And the sense of isolation and abandonment that you feel is only made more extreme by several other considerations which we rarely think about in the rush and excitement of the initial creative process as we're building the business.

Nobody Tells Ya Nothin'

For one thing, which I'm trying to partially address right here, while there's a vast amount of reading and writing that's readily available concerning every aspect of launching a business, there's almost nothing you can turn to for help when your business is headed south. People are fond of saying that, if you want to be there at the landing, you've got to be there from the launch. But the truth is that you're largely on your own when things go wrong because no one wants to be there (much less talk about it or plan for it) when the business is about to crash and burn. Plan B's are generally OK. Plan F is nothing anyone wants to hear anything about until it's way too late in most cases to make a difference. It's a lot like the overwhelming lack of interest we see in writing a will or buying a cemetery plot when you're 25.

In addition, many investors and even close advisors who might be able to give you some help and guidance (although usually not more cash) are way too quick to jump ship when your deal gets in trouble and the funding starts to run out. Experienced entrepreneurs (who have been to this movie before) will tell you that this is just another part of the process and that being left in the lurch comes with the territory. But even knowing that this is commonplace doesn't provide much comfort when it's your place that's in the creditors' cross-hairs. When people start to lose their confidence in you, they are driven much more by their fears than by their hopes

The Pendulum Swings Both Ways

Opportunity costs (just like pendulums) cut both ways. At the outset and when you're a star, everybody takes your calls and wants to be your best buddy. As I like to say: "they'll love ya when you're leading and leave ya when you're losing". Everyone quickly seems to have better things to do than to sink additional time and effort into a deal that's moving sideways or backwards. VCs call these companies "the living dead" and can't wait to move on to the next big thing. The attitude today – more and more in light of the massive number of opportunities – is this: "anything that isn't a clear and obvious winner is a loser". I don't think we're gonna change human nature any time soon, but especially for first-timers, it's important for you to know what you can expect from these folks (not much) in hard times. When things get really rough, your partners, managers and best employees will – by and large – give you a better shake than outsiders, but they too have families, obligations and futures that they need to be attentive to and responsible for – and, in another sad, but true fact of life, it's the most qualified who quickly learn that they have other options and alternatives and they're more likely to leave than the rest of the team. But don't worry apart parting with hard-to-find, terrifically talented people. Here's a little secret – save your business first, then restock your larder. Great talent is attracted far more by the opportunity to solve important problems and by demonstrable unmet demand for the business's products and services than by peanuts, perks and promises.

Tune the Team for Tough Times

Talking about the team, there's an old football rule that, if you want to win consistently, you play your best 11 (the most effective and cohesive team) and not your 11 best (the best individual performers). When you're in trouble and picking the people to keep, this is a CRITICAL concern and often a very tough call. You may have to fire your second best salesman to be able to afford to keep the guy who keeps the servers humming. And as much as it feels like you're throwing away a part of your future upside; when you're in survival mode, you need to first make sure that you'll have the funds to have a future at all. Figure out the functions that really permit the stripped-down business to still function and have a shot at success and go with the people that can make that happen. Among other things, you'll very likely find that it's some of your younger and newer employees rather than the older and more experienced ones who are best suited to this type of a struggle.

Kidding Yourself is Not a Competitive Advantage in a Crisis

One of the reasons young entrepreneurs succeed is that they don't know what they're unable to do. In addition, they refuse to allow their actions to be constrained by the limitations of others. As a result, because they didn't know something "couldn't be done", and there were no rules against doing it, they often end up accomplishing things even though they had never been done before. Their ignorance and abundant confidence in this context is a competitive advantage. They think that they can solve every problem with the application of unbounded enthusiasm and great energy. But the world of counselors, creditors, and courts combined with the constraints of a cash crunch isn't a place of unplowed new ground. There are hard and fast and painful rules and procedures that constitute this environment and they're expressly designed to limit flexibility, restrict movement, and slow everything down. Entrepreneurs sell dreams which they often quite honestly believe. But just because something is exciting and has the ring of truth about it doesn't mean that it matches the realities of the situation and the facts on the ground. Saying doesn't make things so and all the confidence in the world won't make up for a lack of cash. As Charlie Brown used to say: "How can we lose when we're so sincere?"

Entrepreneurs are Super Superstitious

Forget your WPO & YPO forums; strategy seminars and trade shows; your PPMs and IPO plans; and all those other "helpful" resources for a while. These kinds of activities are wastes of precious time that you can't afford and they also won't help a bit. But not for the reasons you might imagine. They won't help because the fear of failure is highly contagious and exhibitions of honesty and vulnerability in most cases don't encourage other entrepreneurs to share; they tend to drive them to shut down and disappear. Even guys you've been close business associates with for years and years aren't gonna be there to help you over these hurdles. The sooner you realize this; the more time you'll save and the less disappointed you'll be in your buddies. No one else is really gonna help bail you out or supply the silver bullet – it's all on you.

So what can you do to at least start to prepare yourself mentally (sooner rather than later) for the prospect that your turn in the dunk tank may be right around the corner?

Here're four crucial rules to keep in mind:

1. Don't Wait 'til It's Too Late

As I suggested above, very few people who haven't been through this process multiple times have any idea of how soon you have to acknowledge your problems and start moving to fix them if you're going to have a fighting chance of saving the ship. You think for example that you can always quickly let people go and stop the burn, but you don't take into account issues like accrued vacation pay, severance, continued insurance benefits, expense reimbursements, etc. and every one of these things keeps the money meter running long after the people may have departed. In addition, there's the opposite side of the coin as well – every day that you move closer to running out of cash – but keep operating the business, you're adding creditors and obligations that you're going to need to resolve in some fashion. A scary example (and just one of many) is the issue of unpaid employment taxes, deposits, etc. which can quickly become personal liabilities for management and directors. Trust me; you don't want to go there.

2. Don't Slice the Salami Slowly

If you have to eat a bunch of ugly frogs, it's a good plan to eat the biggest one first. If you're going to try to save the business, the necessary cuts have to be quick and deep and over as soon as possible so the survivors can get back to work and stop worrying that they are the next to go. Trying to save a couple of people or a marginal job or two is the worst thing you can do. It's never easy or pretty, but doing it piecemeal and over and over again is an early death sentence. People do better absorbing one big shock and getting over the loss than they do dealing with the uncertainty of a series of continued small and ineffective cuts.

3. Start Looking for a Salvage Sale

It may be that you've got a great team or a great idea or a cool new approach or something else going for you. The problem is that to win today, you need <u>all</u> of the above plus a bunch of time and cash. And you've got to know how to run an entire business which might not really be what you're great at and – without a bankroll – no one's interested in waiting around while you learn on the job. However, there are lots of companies looking to acquire whole talented teams; to fold in technologies or tools that they haven't yet built for themselves; or even to start an entire division doing what you hoped to do as a stand-alone business. But you've got to start looking as soon as you start to see the handwriting on the wall. Frankly, even a fire sale – especially one that provides going-forward jobs for the folks who hung in there with you – is a LOT better outcome than extending your struggle for a few months and then crashing directly into the concrete wall.

4. Shoot for a Soft Landing

If you're never planning to pass by this way again, feel free to just smash into the wall, bail out and shut the place down, and leave waves of unhappy folks in your wake. But, what goes around does come around and most young entrepreneurs are very likely (especially these days) to want to get back up on the horse and try it again. The ONLY way you will have the slightest chance of doing this is if you preserve your integrity and credibility by trying to do everything in your power to shoot for a soft landing where you leave as few people holding an empty bag as possible. This goes for vendors, partners, employees, customers, creditors and Uncle Sam as well to be sure. Remember that at these times, you riding a very emotional see-saw and constantly teetering between support and blame from everyone around you.

There may not be enough money to make anyone happy or whole, but careful cash management, full disclosure, good timing, and self-sacrifices will go a long way toward at least generating some understanding. Remember that (unlike friends and families) professional investors (and most decent angels) have seen these scenarios many times and know what the possible outcomes are. Shame on them if they didn't make their commitments with their eyes wide open.

But they'll still be checking to see whether you handled a tough situation like a professional. One amazing way to surprise them is to think about an early shutdown and a partial return of their unspent capital. Here's the bottom line: if you can't see a clear path and a way to win; there's very little reason to waste your time and energy (and your investors' money) on trying to lose more slowly. It's never the hills on the road forward that matter; it's how you handle the ruts that tells the real story for the future.

Bottom line: failing to plan for a possible failure shouldn't be confused with people who are planning to fail (a lack of confidence or commitment) and just going through the motions. It's a much worse failing – it's failing to honor the faith and belief that people had in you. There's always more money – your reputation and credibility are much harder to preserve and restore once they're gone.

FAILURE HAPPENS. FOUR RULES FOR DOING IT WELL

As I wrote in the last chapter, failure is a fact of start-up life. And sometimes, sadly, it's the entire company that fails. As much as we don't like to think about failure, it's important to prepare yourself mentally for the prospect that your turn in the dunk tank may be right around the corner.

Here are four crucial rules to keep in mind:

1. Don't Wait 'til It's Too Late

Unless you've been through this before, multiple times, it's almost impossible to know how soon you have to acknowledge your problems and start moving to fix them if you're going to have a fighting chance of saving the ship. You may think that you can lay people off to stop your cash burn, but it doesn't quite work that way. Long after your employees are gone, you'll be shelling out for accrued vacation pay, severance, continued insurance benefits, expense reimbursements and so on.

Then there's the opposite side of the coin. Every day that you move closer to running out of cash but keep operating the business, you're adding creditors and obligations. Unpaid employment taxes and deposits can quickly become personal liabilities for management and directors. Trust me; you don't want to go there.

2. Don't Slice the Salami Slowly

If you're going to try to save the business, the necessary cuts have to be quick and deep and over as soon as possible so the survivors can get back to work. Trying to save a couple of people or a marginal job or two is the worst thing you can do. People do better absorbing one big shock and getting over the loss than they do dealing with the uncertainty of a series of continued small and ineffective cuts.

3. Start Looking for a Salvage Sale

You may have a great team or a great idea or a cool new approach. But to win, you need all of the above plus a bunch of time and cash.

However, there are lots of companies looking to acquire whole talented teams; to fold in technologies or tools that they haven't yet built; or even to start an entire division doing what you hoped to do as a stand-alone business. But you've got to start looking as soon as you see the handwriting on the wall. Even a fire sale--especially one that provides continuing jobs for the folks who hung in there with you--is a *lot* better outcome than extending your struggle for a few months and then crashing directly into the concrete wall.

4. Shoot for a Soft Landing

If you're never planning to pass by this way again, feel free to just smash into the wall, bail out and shut the place down, leaving waves of unhappy folks in your wake. But most young entrepreneurs are very likely to want to get back up on the horse and try again. The only way you will have the slightest chance of doing this is if you do everything in your power to shoot for a soft landing, leaving as few people holding an empty bag as possible. This goes for vendors, partners, employees, customers, creditors and Uncle Sam.

There may not be enough money to make everyone happy, but careful cash management, full disclosure, good timing, and self-sacrifices will go a long way toward at least generating some understanding. Unlike friends and families, professional investors have seen these scenarios many times and know what the possible outcomes are. Shame on them if they didn't make their commitments with their eyes wide open.

One amazing way to surprise them is to consider an early shutdown and a partial return of their unspent capital. If you can't see a clear path and a way to win there's very little reason to waste time, energy, and money on trying to lose more slowly.

Failing to plan for a possible failure shouldn't be confused with planning to fail. Failing to plan is worse: It's failing to honor the faith and belief that people had in you. There's always more money. Your reputation and credibility are much harder to restore once they're gone.

FORGET ABOUT FAILING FAST. IF YOU MUST, FAIL FORWARD INSTEAD

I'm so tired of reading about and constantly being lectured on the virtues of failing fast that I'm beginning to wonder whether the phrase is an embedded Swift Key on mobile keypads, or a built-in slide automatically inserted into PowerPoint and Keynote presentations. But, as I've said many times, there's no fun in failing (See Who Said Failure Was Fashionable?). And it's no badge of honor to lose, although I don't think that, for young entrepreneurs, it's really a case of losing in any event. Because even if you don't win, you learn a great deal-- as long as you're willing to listen.

Just remember that there's nothing noble about noble failures and that even the grandest failures aren't really fatal. They're just opportunities to start again, better and smarter. The truth is that you'll absolutely learn much more from your failures than your successes, although it won't feel nearly as good. And, you never want to quit too soon because, in the startup world, almost everything looks like a failure in the middle. This is why perseverance is so crucial. Things always look grimmest right before success breaks through.

So, I'd like to fire the phrase "fail fast" and replace it with something that to me is a lot more descriptive of the whole experience and the smart way to look at the process. It's not ultimately about how quickly you fail, it's all about the education, the takeaways and specifically about the mistakes you hopefully won't make again. So instead of making sure that you are failing fast, my suggestion is that you try to "fail forward" when things are headed downhill. Learn and gain in the process. Brene Brown says failure is an "imperfect" word because it's never the end of the story if you're smart. Failures turn into lessons and lessons make you better and somewhat more likely to succeed the next time around as long as you're a good listener. (See 3 Tips from Brene Brown About Failing Brilliantly)

Failing forward has all the virtues of failing fast: an awareness of opportunity costs, the ancient wisdom of "stop digging" when you find yourself deep in a hole, and an understanding that seeking the cure for no known disease or finding solutions for non-existent problems is such a sad waste of your energy and scarce resources. But an important distinction is that the idea of failing forward always looks ahead-- gets you right back up on the horse again-- and builds on the useful and valuable experiences of your prior attempts. In addition, if you handle the wind-down like a pro, you will actually make it much more likely that your next deal will be easier to get done because even failing well is an art. (Failure Happens. Four Ways to Do It Well)

Failure is almost never about a clean sweep or a complete restart--there are too many babies in the bath water to just toss the whole thing out the window. It's always an iterative process with lots of triage included. You want to preserve what worked (remembering that someone spent a lot of time and money on your last adventure), you definitely want to hang on to the people who put their hearts and souls into the program, and you want to be humble and smart enough to carefully determine what went wrong and why. Just a word to the wise about that last idea. In the vast majority of cases it will emerge that what bit you in the ass wasn't just something you weren't good enough at or something that you found out that you didn't know how to do.

The cause will be something that you didn't even know that you didn't know (or hadn't thought about) that made all the difference.

The lesson here is that it's the careful research and the customer investigation-- the stuff you do before you start-- that, in the end, will turn out to have the greatest impact on the success of the business. Because real demand and customers are the whole ballgame. Everything else you can hire, fire, fix or improve as the battle progresses but, if no one wants what you're selling, there's no there there.

MAKE CHEAP MISTAKES

There's a world of difference between failing and simply making mistakes. It's critical for entrepreneurs to understand and recognize the difference. I hear people talking about how proud they are that their last business or venture failed. They brag about what a wonderful learning experience it was. But it's all a crock and a waste of breath. Because you only fail when you give up and giving up is something that winners never do. Failing is failing however you paint it and, when you fail, it's game over. So, in my book, only cretins celebrate their failures.

Making mistakes, on the other hand, is absolutely par for the course and something we all do from time to time. It's a sign of a healthy, active and risk-taking business. The fact is that the only time normal people don't make mistakes is when they're asleep. Mistakes are a critical part of growing and expanding your company and, if you're not stubbing your toe from time to time, it means you're not moving fast enough and pushing forward. Skinned knees are part of the process. Rapid growth and constantly changing circumstances are inherently embarrassing – you need to get used to it. A thick skin helps a lot in a start-up because not everything in life is fair.

When I was first starting out several VCs told me that they never invest in businesses founded by lawyers because too many lawyers are more concerned about being "right" than they are about doing the things that are right for the business. They'd rather die than die of embarrassment. But the name of the game is to win, not to be right all the time. Being smart doesn't mean that you make all good decisions – it means that you learn from your bad ones, don't repeat them, and make the best that you can out of them.

There are a few basic rules that will help you be just as successful in navigating the valleys you encounter along the way as you are in celebrating the peaks and high points of the journey.

Rule Number 1 – Make Cheap Mistakes (Fail Fast)

Not everything worth doing is worth doing well. You need to start small on new projects and be ready to scale swiftly or abandon ship as soon as the handwriting is on the wall. But be careful about the process –don't try to do things cheaply that you shouldn't do at all.

On the other hand, sometimes for a small, start-up company, being smart and cheap is the only way to meet the demands of your customers and to keep up with the competition. Even when the customer's demands are bullshit. Here's an example I had from the earliest days of Fed Ex.

We had a relatively new business called kiNexus which was providing thousands of college graduate job seekers' resumes on CDs to employers on a weekly basis so that they could sort and select interview candidates before they got to campus and often from several schools as well. Many of our actual customers were relatively low level HR people from big corporate employers and their jobs were mainly to schedule and support the "real" recruiters and, as you might imagine, they were insecure, demanding for no good reason and generally pains in the ass. Let's just say that they had issues.

Values, Ethics & Failure in the Digital Age

In any case, around that time, anything in business that was time-sensitive and important was beginning to be sent overnight by Fed Ex and apparently the more Fed Ex packages you got, the more important you felt and appeared to the people sitting around you in your office. So one day in our little business, we started getting regular calls usually on a Thursday afternoon from a number of our customers insisting that they needed their CDs sent overnight Fed Ex (for about $40 a pop at that time) rather than by mail which was costing us 53 cents.

And we started doing it because we wanted to be responsive to our customers even though it was ridiculously expensive and totally unnecessary. And, because we were so conscientious, we'd regularly call the next day to make sure that the package was delivered on time. And guess what we found out? Half the time, the person wasn't on vacation for the next week or wasn't even going to be in the office that day. Most of the time, no one else could figure out what was so urgent about the delivery anyway. And generally, we felt like idiots. But the customer is always right – right?

So here's what we did. We made our own fake Fed Ex envelopes (see below) and we put 75 cents postage on them and sent them regular mail and never had a complaint after that from any of these guys. Ever.

Rule Number 2 – Don't Be Reluctant to Change Your Mind

Nothing in life is written in stone. If you're headed in the wrong direction or digging yourself deeper every day in a hole, the first order of business is to stop. Sticking to the original plan when the conditions on the ground have changed is foolish – you've got to be fast and flexible. To stick with a mistake is actually much worse than making it because delay only compounds and worsens the situation.

Rule Number 3 – Don't Dwell on the Past – Move On

It's always O.K. to admit that you've made a mistake. Make 'em. Admit 'em. Correct 'em. Forget 'em. A short memory and some in-game amnesia are critical. If you're worrying about the past, you've got a good chance of screwing up the future. You can't water yesterday's crops. So move on.

Rule Number 4 – Distinguish Mistakes from Systemic Problems

The best companies understand the very crucial distinction between mistakes (errors that happen once) and systemic problems (errors that happen over and over again) and they make it their business to track and aggregate these occurrences in order to eliminate the root causes of the problems. Mistakes will always happen, but the same mistakes shouldn't happen over and over again – those cases aren't mistakes, they're addressable problems that can be made to go away.

Rule Number 5 – Be a Big Boy or Girl

Don't try to hide a mistake or cover it up – admit it and get to fixing it. Show some remorse and make sure that people know you're taking it seriously. Let the appropriate people know it won't happen again. Don't waste your breath blaming others – you'll need it to say "I'm sorry". Take your medicine – don't sulk – just get back to work and get over it. And finally, don't ruin a good apology with a crappy excuse.

DON'T WASTE YOUR TIME CHASING PERFECT

Not everything worth doing is worth doing to the nth degree. Just like you can overthink and over-engineer your technology, you can foolishly try to achieve levels of immediacy, proximity and precision that frankly no one really needs or cares about--except maybe a few of your geeky engineers. Pursuing perfection is a perfectly good way to burn through lots of cash, waste a lot of time and energy, and frustrate your own people in the process.

In the real world, good enough is often good enough. Trying to be better than that, or perfect, is more about your own neuroses or bragging rights than an attempt to address the actual needs, requirements and desires of your people, users or customers. The Six Sigma standard needs to take a step or two back because; while it's a great goal and a significant standard to shoot for in some businesses and contexts, it's a foolish fantasy and a false formula in the majority of cases.

Constant observation and measurement, ongoing review and iteration, and continuous improvement are essential to your long-term success. But getting too far ahead of your skis, spending more than you can afford shooting for levels of unnecessary precision, setting standards that make no sense and add no value to your offerings, or trying to address too broad a set of needs and customers are formulas for expensive failures. Worse yet, these ever-elusive objectives distract you, diverting attention and resources that need to be focused on far more critical needs.

It's way too easy in our metric-driven digital world to fall in love with stats and factoids and to pursue the numbers while losing sight of the end game. I remember long arguments with clients in one of my first businesses, where we tracked customer satisfaction by making millions of phone calls each year to consumers at home to determine how satisfied they had been with a recent experience. It might have been a service visit, a sales encounter, a meal or a hotel stay.

The clients (and their internal bean counters) were always worried about the numbers - how many interviews had we done, how many were fully completed, how many customers were happy or unhappy. And, believe me, I know those were important considerations. But what they never understood was that the most important measurement-- the real goal of the effort-- was to successfully connect with and, if necessary, "fix" the customer. It was critical to show them that the reason for the call was because we cared about them and their satisfaction-- not that we needed to be sure that our CSI or NPS scores were up to snuff. And, even more importantly, that we would try to resolve any problems or issues they had. If we were interrupting something important, if they just didn't have time to talk, if they didn't care to participate, the critical action was not to push them or browbeat them into participating so we "completed" the interview. The proper thing was to politely apologize for bothering them at a bad time and hang up. Getting it right (not pissing the customers off) was more important than getting one more incremental interview done.

We see similar problems when IT departments exceed their brief and try to achieve levels of company-wide information access without balancing the potential risks to the business against the actual (not imagined or assumed) users' needs. Trying to create and maintain ubiquitous data solutions can create unnecessary exposures from a cyber security perspective without adding any incremental operational benefits. The truth is that all of the people almost never need access to all of your data, and especially not all of the time. This is the constant tension between "real time" and "right time" access that too few companies take the time to understand and manage.

One of my favorite examples of how businesses are exposed to peril is the practice of giving employees working remotely real-time access to inventory, shipping and billing records on the company's main computer systems. Email and collaborative work groups are obvious instances that demand real time access and therefore present serious continuing risks--especially because overall employee compliance and security diligence generally still sucks. Yet there are other important, but less well-understood, areas where catastrophic business invasions, data and financial manipulations, and ransom lockups and accompanying demands are just as likely to arise.

The more frequent exposures and most serious breaches in these areas come through the most mundane of access points. Even worse, the entire business tends to assume that there are no exposures of consequence inherent in the activities around such basic processes. The facts are clearly otherwise and we hear every day about outside penetrations in which company and customer data is stolen, company funds and materials are misdirected and diverted, and millions of dollars of false receipts and invoices are created and fraudulently paid. All right under the noses of the company's financial and audit teams.

But there are some fairly simple solutions and almost every business can figure out a method within their SOPs to take a step or two back from the newest frontier and focus on protecting their basic business instead. And here's a flash: you as the boss need to worry about this because your IT guys are all about the latest and greatest and fastest and they will quickly lead you off in the wrong direction if you don't aggressively rein them in.

They know that it only takes one security hiccup to bring the house down on their heads and they know that such a breach is fairly inevitable and that, at best, they can only play for a tie anyway against the bad guys. So they spend their time focused on the things they can control (and "improve") like access, speed and response times even if the net effect is to increase the company's exposure to external threats.

But you can do better than that and greatly improve your company's odds of avoiding a data disaster. And you can do it quickly and without spending a lot of time or money. There are a bunch of approaches like air gaps and sneaker net systems, but I'm just going to focus on the one I've used successfully in the past which I call the DMZ approach.

To build your own DMZ, you start by asking, who outside your four walls needs access to your internal data and servers, why they need it, and how immediately they need it-- both in terms of access and in terms of the timeliness of the data they are trying to get. What you will find is that a lot of people need little or no immediate access (if they ever need it at all) and that a lot more people can live very happily with levels of access and immediacy that get the job done for them without exposing or jeopardizing any of the company's critical servers and systems. Once you scope and scale the problem, building a straightforward solution is simple.

In our case(s), we knew that we had hundreds of sales and support people in the field and they needed to make regular inquiries. BUT they rarely needed the information they were seeking to be real-time data. It was totally acceptable for more than 95% of the inquiries for specified data to be delivered same day-- not last second. And so, we built the DMZ, which was just a disconnected data repository into which we dumped, and regularly refreshed, relatively current data up to 8 times in a 24-hour business day. Everyone in the field could access that data any time, but those inquiries were never connected or attached in any way to our in-house servers. They had sufficient and timely information to respond to their needs and their customers, and we had a one-way, bullet-proof system that never let the outside world directly access our systems. Everyone in the place slept better and no one was really any the wiser or missing anything they really needed to do their jobs. You should ask the same questions of your own systems before you have your own breach.

Bottom line: even if we could give everyone on the team perfect information in real time and at all times, we couldn't afford it and it wasn't worth the attendant risks. Good enough to get the job done is good enough.

IT'S NOT ABOUT FAILING, IT'S ABOUT SCALING

It's a little depressing at this late date to find that I still have to sit through too many strategy sessions and lengthy lectures with various academics and other "experts" --all of whom sit safely on the sidelines with no skin in the game-- being told what tentative investors we Midwesterners are.

They insist on lecturing us about the definitive difference between East and West Coast investors and us: that we're way too conservative in our investments and too hesitant in our risk-taking. We try to be polite--that's another Midwestern fault, I guess-- while they conveniently ignore recent reports that almost half the venture investments in Chicago have yielded 10x returns.

Apparently, we still haven't learned the wisdom of failure and we're just way too afraid to fail. Better to play it safe than to be embarrassed by a bad outcome. Never mind that we had $8.2 billion of successful exits in 2015 in Chicago alone. I guess we didn't figure out that it takes a few falls, some badly skinned knees, and a lot of other disappointments before you get to grab the brass ring. We've failed failure.

The fact is, there's nothing all that difficult to figure out about failure; we get it. It's an easy knock on the world outside the Valley, but it's no longer one that relates to the new realities and the Rise of the Rest. Dealing constructively with different kinds of failure is a topic I've covered before. Failing, and learning from it, are essential parts of the startup world and of every decent entrepreneur's life About a million other people have also covered the subject, so it's not exactly a mystery waiting for old Sherlock to come along and set us straight.

But the traditional assumptions about the Midwest and the tried-and-true, very tired stories die slowly, especially if you're a writer who's too lazy to look around and see what's actually happening. Apparently, these people don't believe that we can read or that we've actually observed anything in terms of what it takes to build a successful business, or what approaches have really worked over the last decade or two. Honestly, the way that some Unicorns of yesterday are quickly becoming Unicorpses might even suggest that revenue-first investing, and a wee drop of caution and due diligence, might not be such a bad bet.

We farm boys (and girls) know a lot more about failure and its attendant emotions and painful responsibilities than the feckless frat boys (and girls) on the coasts who fail happily on a regular basis, as long as they're burning through Other Peoples' Money. The list of coastal unicorpses (*Quirky* or *Kitchit* anyone?) continues to grow as their VC backers casually write off hundreds of millions of dollars from grossly overfunded deals powered by OPM. To make things even worse, these deals look increasingly like desperate copycat bets that would never get done elsewhere.

These "go-go-gone" deals wouldn't get a second look in Chicago-; not due to some abject fear of failure, but because even the most amateur analysis would tell you that being the 4th or 5th player in a space that was a marginal business to begin with is simply a stupid idea. But, as Gene Kleiner used to say, venture capitalists will go to any lengths to try to copy someone else's success.

Granted, the Left coast in particular does indeed still have a very clear and specific edge in the "go big or go home" sweepstakes. That's all about the appetite (and, in fairness, actual skill) for rapid-fire scaling and the willingness to make big and some would say crazy bets. Reid Hoffman wrote about this distinction a long time ago, but his observation that, in tech-enabled businesses, "first-scaler" advantage consistently beats "first-mover" advantage still rings true. It's not about failing, it's about scaling.

And it's not simply a one-dimensional equation. The momentum and excitement generated by the player who gets big quick has a clear flywheel effect. It pulls talent, funding and other critical resources to the venture and, even more importantly, takes a great deal of the oxygen (and cash) out of the marketplace that would otherwise be available to copycats and other potential competitors.

There's no other place in the world where a kid who's still wet behind the ears, bankrolled by some of the bluest-chip bankers out there, can with a straight face order 2,000 servers for immediate delivery, and actually be taken seriously. Until a lot more investors elsewhere in the country develop a willingness to commit resources at a level which is a full quantum more substantial than anything they've done to date-- not millions, but hundreds of millions--it's entirely likely that the fabulous moonshots and the monstrous flameouts will remain a phenomena peculiar to the Valley. Inexplicable, even irrational, excess will--rarely-- produce previously unimaginable levels of growth and success.

But here in the heartland, we're OK with that. Here, money doesn't lead, it follows and the true capital in new businesses isn't money, it's ideas. If refusing to run through someone else's money like it's water while you figure out whether you're building a real business or backing a bozo makes us conservative or too wary, we're proud of the label and don't mind a bit being painted with that brush. In the end, it's never really about the money anyway. Money is just what people without talent or passion use to keep score. In Chicago, we prefer revenues and results.

TWO WORDS EVERY INNOVATOR SHOULD KNOW

The most important rule of communication in business is a simple one. Say what you mean and mean what you say. Call it honesty, integrity or authenticity – the name doesn't matter, but the language you use and your willingness to honor and abide by your commitments makes all the difference in the world. A mixed or muddled message or a lack of support and follow-through can make everyone miserable and mean the difference between success and failure for your company.

Making and measuring meaningful metrics matters. Alliteration aside, there's no area where this kind of precision and diligence is more critical than in managing the process of business innovation. You need concrete criteria which are objectively determined, fairly applied, and precisely reported. And these need to be aggressively implemented and enforced without exception. If you get the message right at the get-go, you're golden and, if you screw it up and get started on the wrong path or with the wrong attitudes and approach, then you're gonna have a very rough ride and end up nowhere. Frankly, if you don't care where you're going, then any road will take you there.

One of the reasons we little guys win so often these days at least in the short run (and a central theme of the whole disruptive innovation theory) is that, as companies grow larger and more established, their value sets change and they no longer have the necessary flexibility and entrepreneurial attitudes that it takes to get things done.

The "grown-up" core values at a large corporation these days might look like these:

GROWN-UP VALUES	INNOVATION VALUES
Fairness	Fierce Focus
Respect	Ready, Fire, Aim
Opportunity	Good Enough Is Good Enough
Security	Make Many Mistakes
Inclusion/Diversity	Fail Frequently

while the values that drive a successful culture of innovation are more like the ones in the second column. The truth is, as the Bible says (Matthew 6:24), that: "No one can serve two masters". Or, as I'm pretty sure Confucius must have said: "Man who chases too many rabbits catches none".

But aside from the values issue, the real key to successful and ongoing innovation is an understanding of the two concepts which really define the process: "mistakes" and "failures" and the critical differences between the two. Understanding and discussing these two ideas correctly in every conversation you have about innovation is crucial to the focus, clarity and momentum of the process.

If your culture makes your people afraid to talk about the likelihood of making mistakes, you're never going to succeed because, if we knew these things were all going to work out fine, they wouldn't be tests and experiments – they'd be sure things and, just like at the horse races, sure things are safe and comforting, but don't pay squat at the window when the race is done.

So you need to make it O.K. to make mistakes just as long as they are quick and cheap and that you learn from them and – most importantly of all – be sure that they're original. It's important to make your own mistakes and not repeat someone else's.

The second important part of the "conversation" about mistakes is to appreciate and have a process in place that identifies and categorizes systemic "problems" and distinguishes them from "mistakes". It's a simple rule – a "mistake" which happens at your business over and over again isn't a "mistake" – and it's obviously not random - it's a "problem" that needs to be fixed. But only a tiny number of businesses appreciate this distinction and work to find the specific causes of and cures for the problems that cost them substantial amounts of time and energy and money over and over again for no good reason. Tracking these things down and eliminating them is just as central to improving your overall business processes as any new idea might be. Think of it this way – avoiding the potholes in the first place is a lot smarter and cheaper than getting a good deal from the guy towing your car to the garage to have your tire repaired.

Understanding how to talk about "failures" in the context of innovation is also simple to explain and understand, but hard to consistently implement. The good news is that bad examples are readily available and easy to find. People tend to approach failure in three ways – all of which are wrong:

1. On the West Coast – especially in the venture capital community among people who are almost always investors (and not actual business operators), they "celebrate" failure and call it noble and a badge of honor. In addition to being simply BS, and, even if they were referring to the right concept of failure, to me the idea of a noble failure is an oxymoron. True failures truly suck – there's just no two ways about it.

2. Then you have the folks who just refuse to accept the possibility and/or choose to ignore it which is merely stupid and short-sighted.

3. And finally, you have way too many companies that expect and accept failure and all I can say about them is that companies that regularly expect and excuse failures don't ever try very hard to produce anything else.

And yet, while regularly dumping on all these folks, I talk about and embrace failure all the time. So where's the disconnect? It's all in the language you use.

First and foremost, a failure isn't the end. It may be the best you can possibly do under the circumstances. The real error is when you give up and stop trying. We never complain about failures – they're just approaches and solutions that didn't work at the time. In our world, failure is just another word for education. We try to give our people permission to fail, without an acceptance of failure because, while effort is great, ultimately it really is results that matter and move the needle.

Every entrepreneur knows about the "J" curve which predicts that things tend to get worse for a while before they get better and that's just part of the deal. So expect a bumpy road, but always keep moving the ball forward. Things will get better.

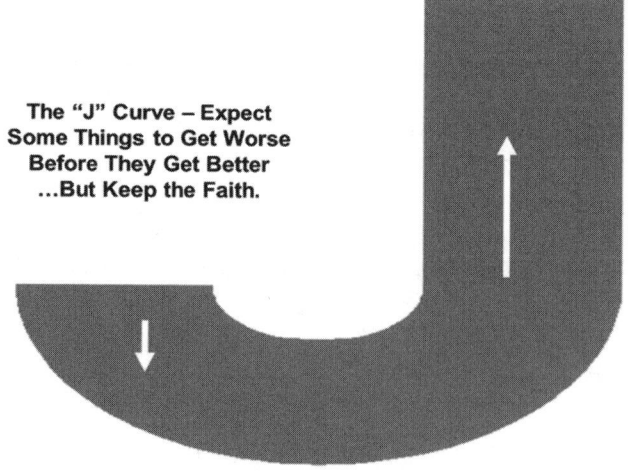

The "J" Curve – Expect Some Things to Get Worse Before They Get Better ...But Keep the Faith.

Our basic mantra is "fail, fail again, and fail better" – each time. And, at the same time, we are merciless about lack of effort or giving up too soon or too often.

The second and most critical part of the "failure" discussion is to focus on "failing fast". If you're in a hole, stop digging. If you're going sideways, bail out. You've got to remember that there's an opportunity cost to everything – whatever you're doing, you could always be doing something else and potentially more valuable to your business. So you've got to be downright greedy with your time which is your scarcest resource of all and very careful about how you spend it.

Saying "no" quickly and often helps immeasurably in this process. There's always too much to do and too many "opportunities" before you – saying "no" is your best strategic tool. And "failing fast and smart" is the methodology that makes this approach work.

TAKE A HARD LOOK AT WHY YOUR STUFF ISN'T SELLING

What "the Boss" Can Teach Us About Loss

If you love Springsteen songs for the lyrics like I do (not that there's anything wrong with the music, of course), and if you're not just sayin' that (like the people who used to claim that they read Playboy for the articles instead of the anatomy), then you know what I mean when I say that there's a line or a poignant phrase from some Bruce song that seems perfect for just about any and every occasion. I can think of dozens of time – staring down into one abyss or facing up to another impending disaster - when Springsteen was the only solace I could find. Even in the worst of times, his music has always been a touchpoint and an anchor to hold on to and, even when you may be at a loss for words, he speaks to all of us.

In This Hard Land, he asks a stranger: "can you tell me what happened to the seeds I've sown…..can you give me a reason, sir, as to why they've never grown?" We've all been there – as entrepreneurs and founders - asking for answers, reasons, or even just explanations to the same recurring questions. And the ultimate answer, of course, is that there aren't any answers – only the road ahead and perseverance. Two ideas which couldn't be more central to Bruce's canon.

An entrepreneur's life is a constant struggle – you're caught each day between sadness and euphoria – teetering between crazy confidence and debilitating doubt – and cranking up one of these ancient anthems is as good an antidote for the everyday angst and the anxiety which we all face as anything I have ever known. The best music takes us to another, better, place – not forever – but long enough to catch our breath, hunker down, and hit it hard one more time.

The truth is that – even if you can't recall the exact language (although a frightening amount of this stuff is stuck permanently in our heads) - you won't have to look very hard to find the specific lyrics on Google which succinctly suit each situation. What's better than chanting the mantra: "no retreat, baby, no surrender" when the going gets really rough? No metaphors required – the meaning couldn't be plainer or more direct – yes, Travis, he's talkin' to you. And it feels pretty good to know that you're not alone in the struggle. There's always someone standing there if you should falter. Crank up the live version of *If I Should Fall Behind* and say no more.

Bruce is, without a doubt, an oracle for the ages (past and present), a master storyteller for our time, and an entrepreneur as well. Every entrepreneur knows in his or her heart exactly the kinds of battles, compromises, and heartaches which he speaks of in his music. His songs describe and fit our feelings (and our failings) like a glove. The connection is similar to (but more emotionally powerful than) the way we interpret the text of every fortune cookie and each day's horoscope so that it feels like it was meant just for us. Listening to Springsteen lyrics is like re-reading a specially-meaningful verse of gospel, an inspirational letter from a long-time friend, or a final farewell note from an old flame.

The Boss can sum up in a few authentic and heartfelt words what it seems as if we've spent a lifetime living and are living every day as well. The songs skip right over all the filters and all the defenses and get right down to the fundamentals. They're perceptive and pithy without being patronizing or pretentious. Philosophical without ever being pathetic. Wise, but never whiny. Short, but oh so smart. And, as he hopes in *No Surrender*: "We learned more from a three-minute record, baby, than we ever learned in school." He's written the uber-text for our lives. And, it's virtually inescapable.

As 2016 draws to a close and we meet each week with dozens of the entrepreneurs who are building their businesses at 1871 to review their progress and their prospects, the Springsteen songs often act like shorthand in my head for the different (and often difficult) stories we're hearing. The successes we're seeing are easy to categorize and to deal with – up and to the right – double down on what's working and kill the dogs - and let's see a lot more of the same. They're - *Born to Run* – all day long.

But the much harder conversations are with the folks who are just treading water and trying to keep their heads above the waves; those whose businesses are going sideways with no positive changes on the horizon; or, worst of all, the ones running out of cash, customers and runway. It's never easy in these talks to say what no one wants to hear. But telling the truth comes with the territory and there are only a few ways – none especially kind or polite – to deliver the bad news.

A product that doesn't sell or a service that no one wants or needs isn't the basis for any kind of successful business. It may be a good feature, an attractive add-on, or a lot of other things, but it's clearly not a company in the making. And the sooner that message sinks in, the better for all concerned. It's always about time, alternatives and opportunity costs and the clock is always ticking.

At times like these, the entrepreneurs' own frustrations and disappointment are also more than obvious — they're palpable. And these folks feel like they've let the whole world down. Bruce said it best in *Jungleland*: "…they reach for their moment and try to make an honest stand but they wind up wounded, not even dead." But the very best entrepreneurs, the ones we'll hear from again, rise to the challenge. They're dangerously honest and, at the end of the day, they don't argue with the facts or the truth. It's as hard to tell the truth as it is to hide it – maybe harder.

It takes a great deal of strength, confidence and courage to stop the frantic, full speed ahead, charge (with you in particular running willy nilly down the road) so you can honestly take stock of where things in your business actually stand. It usually takes a lot more guts to pull the plug at the right time (for everyone's sake) than to keep beating a dying horse. And make no mistake – it's also an obligation you may owe to a lot of other people. Startups don't stop until the founders give up, but sometimes stopping and moving quickly to salvage whatever you can is the smartest thing to do. Even in the darkest hours, Bruce would say that you gotta believe that there are *Better Days* ahead. Leaving the past behind is the first real step to a brighter future.

And now's a very good time to ask yourself the hardest of questions.

The process starts by acknowledging a pretty simple reality: that ultimately the marketplace decides everything. It's not what you want to sell that matters; it's what the world wants and is willing to buy from you that makes all the difference. Businesses aren't generally paid to change or reform their customers; they're paid to satisfy their needs. There are a million excuses, explanations, and other ways to avoid the question, but ultimately customers buy for their own reasons, not yours. They may say they love you – but they vote with their dollars, not their hugs. It's actually pretty easy to keep score and know the difference.

So if your stuff's not selling – even if you are the greatest salesperson in the world and could sell shoes to a snake – or talk a dog off of a meat wagon - then you have two choices: sell something else to the customer or stop selling to the customers entirely and start thinking about selling or shutting down the business. Tech startups and digital businesses in general don't typically have a lot of hard assets to sell (especially in distressed circumstances), but there's still plenty of potential value to be realized (for you and your investors) if you go about the process correctly and so long as you don't wait until it's too late. Knowing what you've got to sell is just as important as knowing when it's the right time to sell.

But it all starts with being honest with yourself. I think of a line from *The River*: "Is a dream a lie that don't come true or is it something worse?" I realize that dreams die hard, but living a lie is harder still. If you tell the truth, it becomes part of your past. If you lie, it becomes part of your future.

BRENE BROWN AT 1871 FOR A FIRESIDE CHAT

We hosted a tour and an hour-long fireside chat for Dr. Brene Brown at 1871 this week as part of our WiSTEM program which focuses on 1871's female entrepreneurs. The event was attended by about 300 excited members of the *Rising Strong* community. Brene was careful at the outset not to call them "fans" although you couldn't prove that from the emotion and energy of the crowd (which started gathering an hour before the sold-out doors even opened) or from the rousing reception and standing ovation she got when she walked on stage. She pointed out that - while her process was a shared experience, a collaborative conversation, and, most importantly, a two-way street – fandom was a fundamentally passive, one-sided, and static state. Simply buying any book won't make you better – it's in applying the lessons and learnings from the book to your own life and circumstances - and then doing the hard work of taking responsibility for and true ownership of your stories - where the change starts and the results begin to show. You've got to put your heart where your mouth is and let yourself be seen.

To say that the crowd was present and "in the moment" would be an understatement. They were absolutely hanging on her every word. But, interestingly enough, at least in Brene's terminology, they weren't being "mindful" which she said was a fuzzy and fussy word that she'd done her best to successfully expunge from her vocabulary. We agreed that a better and more concrete phrase would be that they were "paying attention" which I believe is the newest and most meaningful form of currency today – especially given our noisy, cluttered and confused world. The truth is that, if your audience isn't listening and paying attention, it doesn't really matter what you're saying or selling. And, of course, it turns out that whatever it is that you pay attention to in your business and/or in your relationships are the only things that matter anyway in the final analysis.

Dr. Brown joined us to talk about *Rising Strong*, her newest book (which – a week after publication - is already on the *New York Times* best seller list), and also to talk about a major new online learning and sharing initiative (called *COURAGEworks*) which she will be launching in a few months with Oprah and others. And she was gracious enough to spend some time listening to testimonials and answering questions from the crowd. We covered a lot of territory in our talk, but a few key concepts and ideas stuck with me which I think are particularly relevant to entrepreneurs who are starting new businesses in uncharted waters where the perils are high and the prospects of failure are great.

The most fundamental idea, of course, was the whole basis for the research and the new book itself which was an attempt by Brene to discover what the common qualities were among those who had set out on a journey, failed once or twice, sometimes spectacularly, but who had then picked themselves up, started forward again, and ultimately succeeded. What did it take for them to make it and what attitudes and characteristics did they share? I'm not going to try to answer a book's worth of inquiry in a brief blog post, but here are 3 of the main things that I took away from our talk which – not entirely surprisingly – aligned pretty nicely with some of the central *Perspiration Principles*.

(1) Failure's Just Another Word for Education

I've said for a long time that failure sucks. See http://www.inc.com/howard-tullman/who-said-failure-was-fashionable.html. People who pride themselves on their record of repeated failures are sadly deluded and just kidding themselves. They need to face the facts and face reality so they can get on with their real lives. See http://www.inc.com/howard-tullman/what-nobody-tells-you-about-failure.html. And Brene also made a very interesting comment early in her remarks. She said that "failure is an imperfect word" because, if you take the time and have the patience to learn from your failures, then they aren't failures any longer – they're lessons. See http://www.inc.com/howard-tullman/failure-happens-four-ways-to-do-it-well.html. And once you've gone through the ringer, and learned your lessons – good and bad – it's highly likely that you're a better bet for the next time around. Not a sure thing – but a decent bet. See http://www.inc.com/howard-tullman/should-you-hire-failed-founders.html. What you learn finally is that, if you really own your own stories, you're the one who gets to write the happy endings.

(2) It's Ultimately All Up to You, But You Can't Do It Alone

No one does anything important these days by themselves and having a team to support you and a community to surround you are both critical. And you'll need someone in particular to connect and share with as well. Brene suggested that in her case all the breakthroughs involved a therapist (which we can't all afford although she noted that there are low income programs and practice requirements). And she said that regardless of who you select, there were two more very important caveats: (a) make sure that your happiness and healing doesn't depend on or require their response and/or approval; and (b) make sure that the relationship is truly reciprocal if you expect it to and want it to last. It can't be a one-way street and you can't really open up to someone and share your feelings if the feeling's not truly mutual.

But it's equally critical to remember that – in the end – it's still on you alone to get the process started and the right things done. I tell entrepreneurs all the time that they shouldn't try to convince themselves that they're doing what they are doing for someone else. It's just too hard and long a journey. You need to own the entire process – all the ups and downs – and you need to do it without reservation – putting your whole self out there - because there are no guarantees and there's no halfway way to do what needs to be done. You need to own it and own up to it. All the advice and wisdom in the world won't help until you internalize and take on the task. You can explain things all day to people, but you can't understand for them.

(3) It's Not Always Nice, But It's Always Necessary

The truth is that it's never easy to say what people don't want to hear. But it's an essential step in the communication and sharing process. A leader needs to tell the team what he or she expects of them; what they're trying to accomplish, why it matters, and what sacrifices the journey will entail. Only then - with the requisite knowledge and understanding in place - can everyone sign up and engage with a whole heart. People don't necessarily care that they aren't certain where things are going, but they know for sure that they don't want to go there alone. They want people by their side who share their vision, their passion and their commitment.

But – at the same time - no one can climb the mountain for you and it's critical to understand where you stop and where the others begin. Brene said that empathy is a valuable and important emotion, but it's not an instance of feeling <u>with</u> someone else, it's about your non-judgmental feelings <u>for</u> someone else and their circumstances or situation. And it's that stepping back and creating a bit of distance that makes it possible to help without falling into the pit (or swallowing the problem) yourself. Getting mixed up in the mess isn't going to help anyone. This is why clear limits help to make for a clear conscience and a happy heart.

It's important to be very direct about boundaries (even with family) and, frankly, as Brene said: vulnerability without boundaries – without telling even those you're closest to – what's OK and what's not – isn't vulnerability at all. In the startup business world, everyone wants to help and their enthusiasm is a blessing, but too many people in the process makes for a big mess. Some people just don't get to dance every dance and make every meeting even if their feelings get hurt. That's just another part of the leader's job – ultimately someone has to decide and only that vote counts because it's not a democracy and it's not a popularity contest either. There's no question that how you do it matters a lot, but you've got to do it for sure.

Join the 24 million other people who have watched Brene's TED talk on The Power of Vulnerability: https://www.youtube.com/watch?v=iCvmsMzlF7o .

FIRST THINGS FIRST – FAMILY AND FRIENDS

There are degrees of everything – very few things in our world today are absolute. The amount of regular attention we pay to various matters and things; the extent of our patience for our loved ones, peers and others; and the wide range and intensity of the up-and-down feelings we experience at home and at work every day are all highly variable and emotionally-charged elements of our lives. If variety is the spice of life; it's equally an unsettling, challenging and countervailing offset to the security and stability that we all also relish.

At the same time, some things <u>are</u> for sure. You can't be all things to all people; you can't dance every dance; and throughout your life, you've got to make some hard choices, lots of sacrifices, more than a few compromises, and then you've got to live with them through thick or thin for a very long time. The truth is that you can't really hedge your bets when it's your life and the really important parts of it on the line. We become the sum of our choices over time and those choices determine the kind of person we end up being and how the world sees and values us.

What we become isn't a necessary result of fate or destiny. It's certainly not foretold or pre-ordained in any sense just as there are no guarantees when you start a business. And I don't believe that it's beyond our control and our ability to bend and shape the outcomes to match our desires if we consciously, actively and continually apply ourselves to the task. Throughout our lives, we remain a work in progress. Iteration isn't just a business process; it's a strategy for a life well-lived as well. And the good things that we all hope for don't happen by themselves; you've got to pay attention and make them happen.

One of the most critical choices you'll need to make when you start out in your career is exactly what kind of person you want to be. I think it's somewhat back in fashion these days to be a workaholic. For some of us, it never went out of style. Almost everyone today wants to be an entrepreneur; build a business; and be a big honking overnight success. But that's only part of the story. Just as we say at 1871 that ultimately it's not about making money, it's about making a difference; it's also about more than making a living – it's about making a life. And the "you" you become is a big part of the life you build outside the office right alongside your business.

It's really important - in the frenzy of the work and the world - that you don't lose your sense of purpose, perspective and proportion and risk losing yourself in the process. Your business and your work will always be what you do. These things are not who you are. And it's critical right from the start that you not confuse or conflate the two. This isn't as easy to manage as you may think. Today too many of us worship our work; we work at our play (fitness uber alles); and we play at what little worship we make a part of our lives. Where're the soul and the value in that? And – assuming that we want to – how exactly do we get ourselves back on top of things before they veer entirely out of control?

To handle the constant barrage of useful information, occasional insights and useless chatter as well as the increasing assault on all of our senses and, in fact, just to get successfully through the day; we need a new plan. You can drown in many ways today - in data, in documents, in deliberations and in endless discussions. So, the fact is that we each need to develop new skills (for managing both the data <u>and</u> the people in our lives) which probably most resemble the triage process in any emergency room. It's all about radical and rapid choices – as always – but there are many different kinds of choices in the mix.

At work, we tend automatically to focus on the fiercest fires and the highest flames. We let a great deal of how we spend our days and how our attention is directed be driven by the newest crisis rather than remaining in some kind of control and attending to the critical things that really matter. Attention is a slippery substance (a lot like mercury); easily and quickly redirected and readily dissipated. If no one is paying attention to the right things and the things that count, people just stop caring. Once you stop paying attention to the people in your business that are important and they stop caring about you and your business; they'll go someplace else to find someone else who does pay attention and who does care. It's just a matter of time. But that's mainly the business side of the equation.

As the number of physical, mental and emotional inputs we absorb each day continues to increase; our attention spans are shrinking and it's easy to fall back on systems and formulae and – before you know it – just by force of habit and circumstance, we're applying the same approaches and mental checklists that work so well at the firm or in the factory to our friends and families. This is where things can go very wrong very quickly. Because some of the people decisions we're confronted with every day aren't mathematical or subject to standard rules and procedures – they're choices about others, about feelings, and about our relationships. These concerns are fundamentally different, non-mechanical, and far more complex and they defy easy explanation. People aren't products, positions or policies – they're our co-workers, friends, and family. There's no fixed formula for getting these things right.

But it's just as much our job and equally incumbent upon us to decide all day long what's truly important in these inter-personal instances - both in the moment and in the long run – and to spend the time and direct the required attention to making sense of these situations with the same passion and energy that we apply to our business problems and concerns. It's a given that there's never enough time in the day (and that's never going to change); there's never enough of any one of us to go around (cloning may help this someday); and it's way too easy to find an excuse rather than finding the time to deal with these issues.

But here's the bottom line: your family (when you have one) will be a much more important extension of yourself than any work you do. There's always more work - you only have one family. And, believe me; good friends are also few and far between. Friends are the family that you get to choose – they're hard to find; even harder to leave; and impossible to forget. So as you make 'em; make a plan to hang on to them. They're as important an investment over time as anything else.

Take a little time now to decide how you'd like things to turn out when you look back in 50 years at your accomplishments, your family, and what you've built. It's all right there before you; it's all possible at the moment; and ultimately it's all about what you're going to make of it.

EVEN SUPERMAN GETS SAD SOMETIMES

It may be the season to be jolly and it's always great to celebrate our successes, but as the end of the year draws near, it's also a time to reflect on all the things that didn't get done; the ones that didn't go the way we planned; and even those dashed dreams that turned out to be more about heartfelt hopes than high-value ventures. As frenetic and frazzled as the holidays can be, they're also a great time to take the time to catch your breath, take stock (no pun intended) and look ahead.

During the rest of the year, when you're up to your ears in alligators and everything's a fire drill; it's easy to lose sight of the long game and the real objectives of the business as well as the goals that you've hopefully set for yourself as well. Those personal goals are every bit as important as anything you've got planned for the business. Your greatest fear should never be that you might fail in a given business – there's always another one of those around the bend just waiting to be started – it's the fear that you might spend a significant part of your life working on something that doesn't really matter or make a difference.

You've only got a certain number of "at-bats" in life and it's important to make sure that you make each and every one count for something and that – in the process – you become someone to be counted on as well.

All of this – the ups and downs - the good news and the bad – are part of the deal every entrepreneur makes when he or she sets out to change things. Change is never easy and overcoming the resistance to change is a lifetime job. But like everything else in life, it's all about what you make of the situations you find yourself in and how you move forward that ultimately makes the difference.

This can be a time of rebirth, re-dedication and renewed commitment or you can waste your time and energy doubting yourself, blaming your circumstances (or the folks around you), and fearing the future. Things aren't ever as good or as bad as we imagine and the things we imagine are always worse than the things we face up to and take head on. You can let yourself get down or you can get busy.

I expect that you know where I come out on that question. So I've got three simple suggestions of things to do when you're getting down.

(1) Get Past the Past as Soon as Possible

Don't waste a lot of time looking backwards. There's not much you can do today to change the past, although you can certainly learn from it. Just don't get stuck there because it's almost always an invitation to spend your time navel gazing, making excuses, and bemoaning bad breaks. That's absolutely not where you need to be focusing your energies. In addition, by this late date, I'd expect that whatever lessons there were to be learned from past triumphs and pratfalls have already been incorporated into your going-forward plans. Sitting around worrying about missed chances and blown deals won't help you move the business ahead. You can't build your future on regrets and "shoulda, woulda, couldas." And finally, looking in the rear mirror is distracting. It makes it easy to run off the road or smack into something big and ugly that could have been avoided if you had been looking straight ahead.

(2) Call on Your Customers While You Still Can

Get off your butt and get out there and talk to your customers before they find someone else who's demonstrably more interested than you are in what matters to them. Listen carefully to what your customers are doing and saying about their own pressing needs and their current desires. Customer expectations are progressive. If you're not on top of these needs, you'll soon be at the bottom of their list. Business plans and strategy sessions are great, but if all that effort is taking place in a vacuum uninformed by real customer feedback, then it's a waste of time. There's a great big world outside the four walls of your business and you need to get out there because that's where your future will be found. Remember, you'll never get straighter answers to your questions than the ones you get directly from your customers because they're the ultimate users of your products and services.

(3) When You're Thinking About Quitting, Remember Why You Started

There was an important reason you started your business and a problem or problems you set out to solve because you thought you could make a difference by doing things that hadn't been done before in new ways. When times get tough, you need to remember that it's a marathon and not a sprint and the most critical thing you can do is to keep moving.

I'll bet those problems haven't dried up and disappeared although your approach to solving them may have changed – ideally for the better – and that's O.K. – as long as you're still addressing concerns that remain important to your customers and so long as they're still willing to pay a fair price for you to solve their problems for them.

And I'll bet that there are new competitors coming at you from every direction and competing with you in a variety of ways – price, speed, access, ease of use, etc. That's O.K. too and totally to be expected. Your job is to make it as hard on those folks as possible and the best way to do that is to do your business better than anyone else and to do it that way every single day.

But at the end of the day, when you're feeling as low as you can go, you just need to remind yourself of one simple fact: there's nothing in the world that a true entrepreneur would rather be doing than just what you're doing every day. Coming to a place, working on a dream, and doing it with a group of people who are as excited and enthusiastic about what they're doing as you are is the greatest privilege anyone can have and it's <u>you</u> that's making it possible for yourself, but also for all those other folks who are looking to you to lead the way.

It's O.K. to get down – just don't let it show – and don't ever let them down.

SEVEN SCARS MAKE AN ENTREPRENEUR

When most people talk about how difficult and challenging it is to be an entrepreneur, they actually focus on the most obvious things which, frankly, every entrepreneur should already know – how long and hard you have to work, how risky and difficult it is to try to start something new, how unclear and uncertain things are going to be throughout the journey, etc. But honestly, you can learn about any of these things from about a billion different books which are out there dealing with the trials and tribulations of starting a business. None of these concerns should come as a surprise or as anything that the entrepreneur didn't know he or she was signing up for long before they set out on their venture. They might have been kidding themselves about how hard or easy things were gonna be, but they can't really say that they didn't know.

However, it's not these basic bumps in the road that are the make-or-break considerations and the hardest hurdles for entrepreneurs to deal with as they're building their businesses. And they're also not the ones that create the heartaches and those random gray hairs that pop up years before they should in the fullest heads of hair. The toughest and most painful parts of the process are all about two things: personal (sometimes moral) choices and decisions about people. If you haven't had to deal with some of the problems yet, just give it time because you will be dealing with some of them soon enough whether your business is going gangbusters or slipping sideways or headed south.

These really aren't matters of "if"; they're all about "when". Part One of your job is to be ready. Part Two of your job is to decide how to handle each situation. Here's a hint – there will be plenty of tough questions and hard choices as you build your company, but you've only got one reputation.

1. Miss A Milestone

It happens to almost everyone at some point, but it still hurts. It's hard to swallow and even harder to explain to all those folks who thought you walked on water. This is one of the relatively easy situations to handle after you get over the initial embarrassment and wipe the egg off your face. Just explain the situation to everyone (insiders and investors) clearly and quickly and describe the proposed next steps (and concrete solutions) to get the business back on the right track. Don't play the blame game and don't ruin a good apology with excuses. And don't waste too much time dwelling on the past, playing "woulda, shoulda, coulda", or looking backwards. Learn what you can from the mistakes you made and keep moving forward.

2. Break A Promise

In Hollywood, we used to say that the most important rule of all was also the simplest. It succinctly described celebrity, business and life in the movies all in a single sentence: "I'll love you 'til I don't." Similarly, when Steve Jobs would abruptly change his mind and his direction on a project or a product, he wouldn't explain or apologize. He'd just say: "I'm doing what's right for the business right now." Whatever went before was past and quickly forgotten. He had plenty of issues, but (once he was back in the saddle) he had almost no "business" baggage. In tennis or golf, it's called "in-game amnesia". If you're thinking about the last error, you're far more likely to blow the next shot as well.

The moral of these stories is a pretty basic tenet of Startup Management 101. If you're stuck in the past (or bound by your best guesses from back then), you're not going to change the future. Despite our best intentions and best-laid plans, the world keeps spinning and changing and our commitments and even our most sincere and well-intended promises sometimes don't survive the chaos of rapid change and the required responses as well as the back-and-forth that goes on in between and – as often as not – they shouldn't.

None of us has a crystal ball so we can only do the best we can in the moment. Keeping your word isn't some antiquated Victorian virtue or a nonsense notion in today's world of sadly situational ethics, but it's only one very important consideration as you balance and try to triage the onslaught of confusing challenges and "either/or" choices which your business is going to inevitably face. There are no magic solutions or easy resolutions to these dilemmas. All you can do is to do your best under the circumstances.

3.   Tell A White Lie

Sometimes a little inaccuracy can save tons of explanation and many hours of arguments and lectures, but it's a slippery slope. And the sins of omission in this department are just as bad as white lies or taking advantage of the fact that some director, investor, customer or employee just neglected to ask the right questions. It's not on them to tell the truth – it's on you and – you'll learn over time – that the truth only hurts when you don't tell it. No one likes bad news, but everyone in the investment world really hates surprises and the longer you wait to tell someone the right story and the whole story, the more damage you do to the relationship and to your reputation. It's never easy to say what no one wants to hear, but it's often absolutely essential and it's always the leader's job to do the deed and take the heat that's sure to follow.

4. <u>Make A Payroll from Your Pocket</u>

Sometimes enough is enough (even for an entrepreneur) and, as obvious as it may seem to outsiders, it's still never that easy to admit. Dreams die hard, but there are plenty of times when the baby's just ugly and needs to be put out of its misery. There are rarely skid marks in a startup – you hit the wall pretty abruptly when the show is over. And yet, there are other cases when it seems that there's just one more hill to get over or one more sale to make and then the business will be in the clear and on its way. But, as you look around, you realize that you're the only one left in the room thinking about reaching into your pocket for further funding.

If you've got more cash than sense, this is usually a pretty easy decision. But, a much harder choice arises when you have limited funds and you've already bet the ranch and borrowed as much as you can and now you have to choose between competing mouths to feed and one of those competitors is your family's and your kids' futures. Business doesn't get more personal than this and you have to be VERY careful that your ego and your stubbornness don't overcome your common sense and your most critical responsibilities and obligations.

One of the skills that makes someone a great entrepreneur is tunnel vision, but when it's not just you on the cutting edge, you've got to make sure before you jump into a further swamp that it really is a light that you see at the end of the next tunnel and not a big nasty freight train coming the other way. And – like it or not – it's also not a call you get to make all on your own because it's not just your future that you're foolin' with. This is another really hard conversation to have with all of the interested parties, but you owe it to everyone who helped get you started and stuck with you through all the ups and downs to make sure that they're there when the rubber really hits the road and the business hangs in the balance.

5. Give Yourself Some Goodies

Entrepreneurs are basically big crybabies and spend a fair amount of their time feeling sorry for themselves and grossly under-appreciated. They feel taken advantage of, conspired against, and constantly let down by people who don't share their crazy zeal. And I'm just talking about the healthy ones. You can forget about the truly paranoid ones and you'd do well to steer clear of them. A good rule of thumb is to never work for someone who has more emotional problems than you do.

So, you might ask, what does this have to do with you? Well, it turns out that it's a pretty short step from feeling victimized to deciding (in your own addled brain) that you're pretty much entitled to take whatever you can get or get away with. And it always starts small and gets worse over time. And, whether you believe it at the moment or not, you will be there one of these days. It's just another inevitable part of the process. Too much work, too little family time, too much stress, too few strokes – and one day the switch just flips – and the hard choices are staring you in the face.

Expensive meals and travel, hi-tech gadgets and gear you'd never pay for yourself, sports tickets, special events and other goodies for the guys, etc. All "justified" in the name of marketing, morale, and media among other claims and excuses. And all that's basically really going on is that you're taking your company's and your investors' money and putting in your own pocket.

And, believe me, once this bullshit begins, there's no end to the dollars that can disappear and no limit to the rationalizations and outright deceptions that accompany this kind of sick and deluded behavior. Once you start feeling like the business owes you a bunch, it's amazing how quickly that comes to include just about anything you can imagine. Redecorating your home "office", all kinds of loans and advances that never seem to get repaid, cash advances at the strangest times and places, etc.

The truth is that you wouldn't begin to believe the crazy justifications you hear (sadly after the fact and the damage has been done) to explain what any sane person would simply call stealing or worse. You may feel that this shoe will never fit you and that's great. But I'd say it still makes sense to be on your guard and watch your step.

6. Fire A Friend

When you're all sitting around in the garage getting started, it's pretty easy to say just about anything about things to come in the future and (mostly) to convince even yourself that you mean it. And in your heart you probably do, but your head already knows better. "Friends forever" is one of those promises that (in the world of startups) are almost always made to be broken. As time passes and your company grows (and the demands of the real world start to intrude), you'll quickly discover that: (a) you don't get to make all the decisions by yourself any longer; (b) that the needs of the business can quickly outgrow the talents and skills of even the best of your friends and co-founders; and (c) that – like it or not – in building a business and especially a company culture, majority rules. If your closest friend can't cut it with his or her co-workers, you absolutely know who's got to go. That doesn't make it any less painful to disappoint and fire a friend (and you'll find yourself getting mad at the faceless others who are "making" you do it), but – in the end – it's the right and only thing to do for the good of the company. And you need to "own" the decision. Don't complain or tell anyone that "they" made you do it or that you had no choice (even if you didn't) because when you blame these hard decisions on others, you're giving up your own credibility and authority. If it's the right decision and the right call, then it's yours to make and yours to live with.

(7) Do It All Over Again

They say it's hard to go home again and I think that's probably right. But I know for a fact that it's sheer torture to have to blow up your whole business and start all over again. And most people just aren't up to the task – they give it the good old college try, it doesn't work out for them, and then they go get a day job to feed themselves and their families. And there's nothing wrong with that for them – it's just not how it works for a true entrepreneur. And frankly, I'm not sure that you can even call yourself a true entrepreneur if you haven't had to go thru one or two of these near-death experiences yourself.

People that get it right the first time and never have to re-trench or re-load might be the smartest folks around. Or they could just have been remarkably lucky – right time, right place, right investors, connections, etc. For myself, I like to bet on the ones who've been thru the Valley of Death and come out the other side (maybe not smiling), but with their energy unchanged, their passion intact, their commitment strengthened, their teams largely still together, and their eyes always on the prize. They are the scarred and battle-hardened pros that I call real entrepreneurs.

ABOUT THE AUTHOR

Howard Tullman is the CEO of 1871 in Chicago where digital startups get their start. He is also the General Managing Partner of two venture funds: Chicago High- Tech Investment Partners and G2T3V, LLC, which both focus on funding disruptive innovators. He is the former Chairman and CEO of Tribeca Flashpoint Media Arts Academy in Chicago. He is an active member of numerous city, state and civic boards and organizations and a tireless supporter and mentor to many start-ups and other businesses and individuals. He has successfully founded more than a dozen high-tech businesses in his 50 year career and created more than $1 billion in investor value as well as thousands of new jobs. He writes a regular weekly blog on The Perspiration Principles for Inc. Magazine and can be directly contacted:

- by email at h@1871.com
- on twitter @tullman
- his blog: tullman.blogspot.com
- his primary website: www.tullman.com

To get all of Howard's blog posts in one download, visit Blogintobook.com/tullman/.